MW00810405

A Brief Compendium

OF

Bible Truth

by

Archibald Alexander

PROFESSOR AT PRINCETON THEOLOGICAL SEMINARY

Edited by Joel R. Beeke

REFORMATION HERITAGE BOOKS

Grand Rapids, Michigan

For additional Reformed literature, both new and used,
request a free book list from the above address.

PREFACE

God raised up the author of this compendium early in the nineteenth century to help establish the Presbyterian church in America. Archibald Alexander was born April 17, 1772, in a log cabin near Lexington, Virginia, to William and Ann Alexander, staunch Scotch-Irish Presbyterians. He was the third of nine children. As a boy, Archibald loved nature and learning; at age seven, he could read the Bible and recite the Westminster Shorter Catechism. He received a strong classical education in his youth, mastering Latin and Greek at an early age. For several years he studied at Liberty Hall Academy (now Washington and Lee University). His father, who was determined to give him the best possible education, donated land for the academy.

Archibald studied under William Graham, a graduate of the College of New Jersey who had studied under John Witherspoon. Many of Witherspoon's lecture notes were passed by Graham to Alexander and his peers. Later, Alexander expressed appreciation to Graham as a thoroughly grounded classicist and acknowledged that Graham had more influence on his thought and character than anyone else.

Alexander interrupted his studies at age seventeen to become a private tutor for General John Posey's family. He spent much time in Posey's library, reading and meditating. He went through a period of prolonged spiritual struggle with his inherited orthodoxy and new-found understanding of experimental piety, which he observed in Christians. That was reinforced by a tract he found in an old trunk of books, titled, "Internal Evidences of the Christian Religion by Soame Jenyns." Alexander described his impression of the tract: "At every step conviction flashed across my mind, with such bright and overwhelming evidence, that when I ceased to read, the room had the appearance of being illuminated." Alexander was realizing that Christianity was more than an affirmation of intellectual propositions; it was also a personal, experiential relationship with Jesus Christ. His readings and acquaintance with Christians who spoke of the personal work of grace in their lives led him to a new understanding of biblical piety and the role of religious affections in nurturing the Christian life.

During this time, Alexander went to various revival meetings in the Blue Ridge region with his former tutor, Rev. Graham. Despite the revival sermons and the theological discussions in which he engaged, Alexander remained fearful and conflicted about his own salvation. He spent long hours in the woods reading Scripture and praying, yet he could not lift himself beyond "the bitterness of despair." At times he "rolled on the ground in anguish of spirit" over his sins.

Alexander was brought to freedom in Christ in 1789, before he turned eighteen. He had several experiences in which the entire plan of salvation was revealed "as clear as day" to him. He could then believe that "Christ as an Advocate was able to save me." After making profession of faith, Alexander took a new course of studies under Graham, this time in preparation for the Christian ministry. Besides his formal studies with Graham, he had opportunities to travel with his instructor as an itinerant preacher in the early days of the Second Great Awakening.

Licensed to preach by his local presbytery at age nineteen, Alexander received a commission to serve as an itinerant missionary in Virginia and upper North Carolina. His preaching was remarkably successful, resulting in numerous conversions. Itinerant ministry provided Alexander with an understanding of the characteristics of true Spirit-wrought revivals and gave him a life-long passion for home and foreign missions. This was the training ground for his development as a preacher.

Itinerant missionary work eventually gave way to a settled pastorate. On November 7, 1794, Alexander was ordained as pastor of the churches of Briery and Cub Creek, in Charlotte County. Here, too, his work was blessed. Two years later, he accepted the presidency of Hampden Sidney College in Virginia, when he was age twenty-four. Throughout his years of presidency, Alexander preached often in various churches. In 1801 he took a year off to preach throughout New England, where he was exposed to the New Theology of the post-Edwardsean era. His son, James, writes in his biography of his father that this resulted in solidifying Alexander's views "in the direction of the common Westminster theology."

Alexander's growing reputation as a preacher resulted in a call in 1807 to Third (Pine Street) Presbyterian Church, one of Philadelphia's largest churches. Both his preaching and his pastoral work bore much fruit. He established an Evangelical Society that promoted street preaching and two-by-two visitation; he also began the Philadelphia Tract Society and the Foreign Missions Society.

In 1810, Alexander received a doctor of divinity degree from the College of New Jersey. When Princeton Theological Seminary was founded in 1812, Alexander was appointed to serve as its first professor. He labored there for the remaining thirty-nine years of his life, serving mostly as Professor of Didactic and Polemic Theology. At Princeton, Alexander combined three emphases:

- Seventeenth-century Reformed theology—as exemplified in the Westminster standards and in the systematic theology of the Swiss theologian, Francis Turretin;

- Fervent piety and vital interest in genuine religious experience, rooted in revival preaching; and

- Scottish Common Sense philosophy (learned from William Graham), which capitalized on defending the truthfulness of Scripture and the value of Christianity by focusing on internal evidences, such as the self-authenticating and sublime character of Scripture, and external evidences, such as fulfilled prophecy, cultural benefits attending the gospel's spread, and "common sense" perceptions relative to God's existence and natural law.

Alexander was a distinguished scholar and pastor-theologian at Princeton. Entrusted with the responsibility for organizing the seminary curriculum and implementing the seminary's goal to provide spiritual leadership through sound learning and vital piety, Alexander became the fountainhead of Princeton's influence on American Presbyterian churches in the first half of the nineteenth century. Both pulpit proclamation and pastoral practice reflected his ideals and embodied his vision for ministry.[1] Together with his colleague, Samuel Miller, he set a standard of excellence that his successors—most notably, Charles and Archibald Alexander Hodge, Benjamin B. Warfield, and Alexander's own son, James Addison Alexander— studiously maintained.

In his classroom instruction, preaching, and literary achievements, Alexander established himself as a profound thinker and theologian of devotional spirituality. His labors resulted in a number of written works on apologetics, historical theology, biblical history, spiritual biography, and church history, as well as a volume of published sermons. One of the great experimental preachers of his era, he is most remembered today for his publications on practical divinity and spiritual biography.

The present republication of Alexander's *A Brief Compendium* (originally, *Compend*) *of Bible Truth* is a welcome addition to the growing corpus of reprinted material from early faculty members of Princeton. First printed in 1846, this summary of the main doctrines of Christian theology was intended to be a pocket theology for "plain, common readers" who did not have the time or opportunity to study larger works of systematic theology but still wanted to grow in their understanding of the doctrines of Christianity.

Alexander maintained that knowing the "truth in its true nature" is essential for maturation in godliness; biblical truth is the food that nourishes the mind and feeds the heart. Truth is essential to direct religious affections to a God-centered lifestyle in which the Lordship of Christ is expressed in every area of the believer's life. Right living is only possible through right thinking about God and His revelation in the pages of Holy Scripture. In order to think rightly one must have an understanding of the doctrines of the Old and New Testament. This is, as Alexander says in his foreword, the reason why he wrote this book: "Being firmly persuaded that divine truth is to be the grand instrument for the illumination and reformation of the world, he feels desirous to contribute his humble part towards its universal diffusion."

As a precursor to Charles Hodge's later popular exposition of basic Christian doctrines, *The Way of Life*, Alexander's *A Brief Compendium of Bible Truth* is a rich and compact treatment of the primary doctrines of the Christian faith. Although brief, its theological erudition underlies its content. Alexander was well-versed in both the development of historical theology and the contemporary issues that the Christian church was facing in his time. His ability to speak in theological shorthand enabled him to crystallize the important aspects of the doctrines in such a way that his readers could grasp and put into use the essential truths of those "things most surely believed."

Alexander's interest in the practical use of Christian theology is evident, for example, in the judicious remarks he makes in Chapter 24. After warning readers about the dangers of an overly refined orthodoxy, he examines whether faith precedes repentance or repentance precedes faith. Noting that it is impertinent to ask "whether a whole precedes one of its parts, or is preceded by it, [since] no man can give a sound definition of evangelical repentance which will not include faith," he observes that "it is altogether wrong to perplex the minds of serious Christians with useless questions of this sort. Let the schoolmen discuss such matters to their heart's content, but let the humble Christian rest in the plain and obvious meaning of the words of Scripture. The effect of divine truth on the heart is produced by general views, and not by nice and metaphysical distinctions."

This edition includes textual references placed in brackets that are alluded to in Alexander's explanation of various doctrines; those references placed in parentheses are Alexander's own. It also breaks up sentences that may be too long for the modern reader to grasp, and paragraphs that are too lengthy for the modern reader to appreciate. A careful reading of this valuable compendium will more than repay today's reader for the time spent perusing its pages. Though not exhaustive in its treatment, it enables twenty-first century readers to comprehend those biblical truths that matter most for their walk as believers in today's world. Good theology makes strong Christians; growing knowledge of the truth produces godliness for this life and the world to come. At the very least, this book will give today's Christians a better understanding of the spiritual values of another generation who ran the race well and have now entered into their rest, and whose lives and teaching remain as examples for us to imitate in belief and practice.

James M. Garretson
Joel R. Beeke

---

[1]For further discussion on these topics, see James M. Garretson, *Princeton and Preaching: Archibald Alexander and the Christian Ministry* (Edinburgh: Banner of Truth Trust, 2005).

ADVERTISEMENT

At the request of a benevolent friend, the author prepared a brief *Compendium of Bible Truth*, to be inserted in a volume intended for the instruction of the blind, which contained also prayers and hymns to aid their devotions. When this volume was published by the Presbyterian Board of Publication, it was thought this small Compendium might be rendered useful to others, as well as the blind. Accordingly, it was printed in a diminutive volume, which, though it treated on the most vital subjects of theology, might be read from beginning to end in two or three hours. This little volume was published without the author's name. Being persuaded that it might with advantage be enlarged, he has added what increases the volume to more than double the size of the original publication; and this, not by adding to the chapters already printed, which are left unaltered, but by introducing other subjects, not treated in the Compendium as first prepared.

The volume now given to the public comprises a brief system of theology, and may be found useful to such as may not have the opportunity of studying larger works. As it is not intended for the learned, but for plain, common readers, technical phrases and abstruse disquisitions have been avoided; yet the author has attempted to establish every doctrine advanced by solid arguments derived from reason and Scripture.

Being firmly persuaded that divine truth is to be the grand instrument for the illumination and reformation of the world, he feels desirous to contribute his humble part towards its universal diffusion.

So far as Bible truth is contained in this brief Compendium, may the blessing of God attend it to the benefit of every reader. And if anything erroneous has been uttered, may it be forgiven, and its evil tendency counteracted.

Archibald Alexander

CONTENTS

A Brief Compendium

of

Bible Truth

CHAPTER 1

Being of God

Of all conceptions of the human mind, the idea of God is the most sublime. It is not only sublime, but majestic. Everything else appears diminutive while the mind is occupied with this thought. Though the idea of an eternal and infinite being is too great for the grasp of the human intellect, yet it is suited to the human mind. It fills it, and produces a feeling of reverence, which is felt to be a right emotion. If there is no such being, this is the grandest illusion which ever possessed the imagination of man. If it be an error, then error is preferable to truth; for on this supposition, truth in its whole compass has nothing in grandeur to compare with illusion. Remove this idea and the mind is confounded with an infinite blank. Deprived of this, the intellect has no object to fill it; it is confounded and distressed with the retrospect of the past and prospect of the future. But it cannot be that this noblest of all conceptions of the human mind should be false; the capacity of the soul of man to form such a conception is a proof of the existence of a great and good and intelligent First Cause.

God has not left Himself without a witness of His being and His perfections. It may well be doubted whether the evidence of a divine existence, the Author of all things, could be clearer and stronger than it is.

A display of exquisite skill in every organized body around us is far better evidence than any extra-ordinary appearance, however glorious, or the uttering of any voice, however tremendous. Such miraculous phenomena would indeed powerfully excite and astonish the mind, and would be a certain proof of the existence of a superior being; but would, in reality, add nothing to the force of the evidence which we already possess in the innumerable curiously and wisely organized animal bodies by which we are surrounded. And if we were confined to the examination of our own constitution of mind and body, the innumerable in-stances of manifest wisdom in the contrivance of the several parts, their exact adaptation to one another, and their wonderful correspondence with the elements of the external world without us, the evidence of an intelligent cause is irresistible. If any man surveys the structure of the human body, its bones and joints, its blood-vessels and muscles, its heart and stomach, its nerves and glands, and all these parts put into harmonious action by a vital power, the source of which is not understood—if he surveys the adaptation of light to the eye, of air to the ear and to the lungs, and of food to the stomachs of different animals, and notices the exact correspondence between the appetites of animals, and the power of their stomachs to digest that food and that only which is craved by their appetites respectively, and considers what wonderful provision has been made for the preservation and defence of every species—how much wisdom in their covering, instruments of motion and defence; in the propagation of their respective species, and the nourishment of their young—I say, if any man's mind is so constructed as to see all these things, and yet remain sceptical respecting the existence of an intelligent cause, the conclusion must be that such a mind is destitute of reason or has not the capacity of discerning evidence and feeling its force.

In prosecuting the argument from the evident appearance of wisdom in the structure of animal and vegetable bodies, it is not necessary to multiply these cumulative proofs; for as one watch, or one telescope would prove the existence of a skillful artist, so the careful examination of a few specimens of animal or vegetable organization will satisfy the mind, as well as the minute survey of thousands of similar organizations. The attempts of ingenious and scientific men to account for these appearances, so evidently indicative of design, without the supposition of an intelligent Creator, are so replete with folly, that we cannot but think such men abandoned of God to believe a lie, because they liked not to retain the knowledge of God in their thoughts. So it is still true, that it is the fool who hath said in heart, "there is no God" [Ps. 14:1; Ps. 53:1].

If all other arguments for the being of God were wanting, the truth might be inferred with strong probability from our moral feelings. Every man feels himself bound by a moral law; he cannot but see the difference between right and wrong, in many actions. The former he feels to be obligatory, the latter not. Whence this binding internal law, so deeply engraven on the heart of every man, that he cannot escape from the feeling of its obligation? Does it not clearly intimate that there is a Lawgiver, who has provided a witness of His right in every bosom? Where there is a moral law there must be a moral governor. As long as conscience exists in the breasts of men, atheism cannot prevail long. In the tumult of the passions, in the glare of false reasonings, God may for a while be forgotten and His very being denied; but, ere long, these moral feelings will bring men back to the acknowledgement of their Creator. There is good reason to think that the preservation of some religion among all nations is more owing to their moral constitution than to any reasoning on the subject. We need not fear, therefore, that atheism will ever prevail very generally, or continue long.

CHAPTER 2

Personality and Perfection of God

It is admitted by all who believe that God exists that He possesses all conceivable perfection. Right reason would lead us to the opinion that as He is infinite, He must possess attributes of which, at present, we can form no conception. Our ideas of excellence cannot exceed the manifestations of perfection in creation, but it would be absurd to suppose that any excellence could be in the creatures which did not exist in a higher degree in the Creator.

As all men who acknowledge a God agree that all possible perfection belongs to His character, it is unnecessary to adduce any arguments for its proof. Indeed, it seems to be an intuitive truth, that all perfection must reside in the first cause. The very idea of God is that of a being infinitely perfect. Whatever doctrine, therefore, derogates from the perfection of the Supreme Being must be false. It is, therefore, the dictate of reason that we should remove from our idea of God everything which argues any weakness or imperfection. And as our ideas of natural and moral excellence are derived from contemplating the creatures, we must rise to just conceptions of the Deity by ascribing these excellencies to Him in an infinite degree.

Upon this principle, we ascribe to God unity, spirituality, power, knowledge, immensity, eternity, immutability, sovereignty, holiness, justice, goodness, and truth. Upon this principle, God must be independent, and perfectly free to act according to His own pleasure.

God is a person, distinct from the universe. Every being who possesses intellect and will is a person. The execution of any work of design in which there is an adaptation of means to ends, and a harmonious operation of parts to produce a desirable effect, necessarily involves the exercise of both intellect and will. The idea that the universe is God or that God is the soul of the world, but not a person distinct from it, is nothing more than a disguised system of atheism. God is distinct from and independent of all creatures.

CHAPTER 3

The Holy Scriptures

The Bible is made up of many books written throughout a period of more than fifteen hundred years by men who professed to have received their doctrines from God and to have committed them to writing by His direction. These Scriptures, then, must contain a revelation from God, or be a vile imposture. On the latter supposition it is remarkable that the same purpose of deception should be maintained for so long a period by a succession of impostors, all agreeing in the same sentiments, and that the cheat should never have been discovered.

Again, when we examine the moral character and tendency of these books, it is unaccountable that, throughout, they should inculcate a sublimer theology and purer morality than any other books in the world; that they should condemn every species of vice, and especially, that they should severely reprobate all falsehood, deceit, and fraud; thus, in almost every page, pronouncing their own condemnation. As it cannot be explained what could have made wicked impostors wish to inculcate such doctrines, so it is contrary to all experience that men of habitually corrupt minds should be able to conceive or write discourses of so much moral purity and surpassing excellence. Read the sermons of Christ. Peruse the epistles of the apostles, and try to believe that these discourses proceeded from men steeped in fraud and corrupt principles. We are ready at once to say—impossible! When we see light, we know that it must have proceeded from a luminous body. When we see wisdom in creation, we know that there exists a being of incomparable wisdom; and when we read a book of extraordinary power of argument, or replete with sublime imagery, we are sure that such works are the product of gifted minds. What shall we think then, when we behold in the Scriptures moral excellence shining forth in the purest and most comprehensive precepts, and embodied in bright examples of consistent piety and virtue?

The character of Jesus Christ, as portrayed by the evangelists, is itself a moral phenomenon which cannot be accounted for on any other supposition than that the writers were inspired. It is easy in words to ascribe exalted virtues to a hero and to exaggerate his excellences by heaping up pompous epithets; but to describe a character of perfect virtue by merely relating what he said and did, and to place him often in circumstances where it is not only difficult to do right, but where an extraordinary wisdom is requisite to determine what is right, is not easy. But in this way has the character of Jesus Christ been delineated by the evangelists without one word of eulogy. And let it be remarked, that they were unlearned men who had enjoyed none of the advantages of a liberal education. Let any number of common, uneducated men undertake to write a history of some eminent person, and what would be the result, even if their intentions were honest? No honest inquirer can read the Pentateuch, and fail to rise from the perusal, astonished at the wisdom, the majesty, the purity, and the simplicity of the composition. Is it possible then that the five books of Moses are a base forgery? Could an impostor have persuaded a whole nation to adopt a burdensome and expensive code of laws, if he had not been able to give undoubted evidence of his divine mission? And could he have so deluded a whole nation as to induce them to believe that they saw the miraculous judgments of God poured out on the Egyptians, that they saw the sea divided at the word of Moses, that they actually marched through an arm of the sea as on dry land, and that they had been fed with manna rained from the clouds for forty years, and had seen the water gushing from the dry rock upon the touch of the wonder-working rod, if no such events had ever occurred? The history of these miracles is so interwoven with the common events, and with the religious institutions of the Jews, that they cannot be separated.

Let the skeptic tell us what motive could have induced any wicked impostor to write the book of Psalms. Here we have not merely sublime poetic imagery, but a spirit of fervent elevated devotion, to which there is no parallel in all the heathen writings. He must have been a strange impostor that could compose such songs, or could have felt any pleasure in such elevated, spiritual exercises. Can the deist now produce any compositions which will bear a comparison with these?

Again, read the book of Proverbs. Do you see any marks of imposture here? Do we not find concentrated, more useful maxims of prudence and political economy, and more excellent moral precepts than can be gathered from all the sages of the pagan world?

But it may be alleged that men differ in their tastes

respecting the internal excellence of literary compositions, and that in a matter of so great importance we ought to possess some more decisive evidence of divine inspiration. Well, what will be considered sufficient evidence that God has made to men a revelation of His will? Will it be satisfactory if they who profess to be inspired are enabled to do works which are far above the power of man and which require the almighty power of God? No one will doubt that if God give His attestation to any declaration, it should be received as true, for "God is not a man that he should lie" [Num. 23:19].

If then, the apostles actually wrought miracles in the name of Jesus, and in confirmation of their doctrine, it cannot be denied that they were inspired. That such miracles were actually wrought openly and in the presence of watchful and bitter enemies is a matter of record. The four evangelists have testified in the gospels that Christ gave sight to the blind, hearing to the deaf, health to the sick, sound limbs to the cripple, and that in several instances, before a multitude of people, He raised the dead. They testify that after His crucifixion He rose from the dead, and that forty days after His crucifixion He sent down, as He had promised, the Holy Spirit on the apostles, bestowing upon them and others various miraculous gifts, which Paul publicly testifies were common in the churches. The truth of Christianity, then, rests on this single point: Is the testimony of these miracles true or a mere fable? That the gospels were written near the time when these things were done is capable of the fullest proof. Indeed, had not these facts been credited fully by the first disciples, they never would have submitted to such sacrifices and exposed themselves to such dangers as we know they did. All earthly considerations weighed heavily on the other side. Every convert to Christianity is, therefore, a witness of the truth of these miracles; for they had every motive to examine into the truth, and the facts were of such a nature that they could not have been deceived.

It does indeed require strong evidence to satisfy the mind that there has been a departure from the common course of nature, but testimony may be so strong that it would be unreasonable to doubt of the miracles which it is brought to attest. It is admitted that there have often been false witnesses and that we may be deceived by trusting to insufficient testimony, but we also know that in many cases our faith in testimony is as strong as in those things which have passed before our eyes. The point of examination, then, is whether it is more probable that the testimony is false or that a miracle has been wrought. If many persons, without any motive to deceive and without previous concert, agree and maintain in the midst of threatenings and sufferings that they have witnessed miracles, it would be folly to disbelieve. And, especially if such events followed in such immediate and continued succession as can only be accounted for by supposing the miracles to have been performed, the evidence may rise to such a degree of certainty as to assure us that we are not deceived. Now the conversion of the civilized world to Christianity can never be accounted for on any supposition but the truth of the miracles and supernatural influence accompanying the gospel. And the whole train of succeeding events corroborates the truth of the evangelical history.

Another incontrovertible evidence of the truth of

Christianity is the salutary effects it has produced in the world. The conversion and reformation of sinners has been a standing proof of the divine origin of the Bible, and this evidence is not confined to ancient days. Blessed be God, clear and striking instances of the reformation of wicked men have occurred under our own observation. The gospel has produced in our own times such a remarkable change in the moral and civil condition of some of the most ignorant, degraded, and vicious tribes of heathen, that if there were no other evidence of its truth, this would go far to satisfy an honest mind. Can any reasonable man believe that preaching a cunningly devised fable would turn men from their sins, to which they had been long habituated?

Hundreds and thousands in Christian lands can also testify that the truth of God has produced a powerful and salutary effect on their own minds, convincing them of their sin and danger, and exciting in them trust in Christ, which has enkindled their love and brought sweet peace into their troubled breasts. We see, continually, that the power of the gospel affords consolation in affliction and buoys up the soul with assured hope, even in the hour of death.

But if all the convincing proofs abovementioned were wanting, the undeniable prophecies which have been literally fulfilled are a clear demonstration of a divine revelation, for who can predict distant future events but God alone? The prophecies relate to the fortunes of the Jewish people —to the destiny of many great and proud cities and nations; but the most important predictions of the Old Testament relate to the Messiah, which were literally fulfilled in Jesus of Nazareth. Yet no prophecy of Scripture is more striking and

convincing than that of Christ respecting the destruction of Jerusalem, and the ruin and dispersion of the
Jews, the fulfillment of which is recorded in the history
of Josephus, who was not a Christian, but an eyewit-
ness of the facts.

CHAPTER 4

Unity of God

The idea of God is forced upon the rational mind to enable it to account for the innumerable marks of design manifest in the universe, but there is no necessity to suppose more than one great First Cause to account for everything. There is, therefore, nothing in reason or in the works of nature, which would lead to the conclusion that there are more Gods than one. Indeed, the very supposition of more Gods than one shocks and confounds the rational mind. If we were capable of comprehending the subject, it is more than probable that we should see that the existence of two infinite beings is an absurd and impossible conception. There is, however, no need to resort to metaphysical arguments; the harmony of the laws of the universe indicates one mind—one counsel. The existence of evil led some of the ancients to adopt the theory of two eternal beings; but if that were true, we should find two systems of laws in the universe, and a continual interference and collision between them; whereas, the laws of matter, even as far away as the planets and stars, are uniform. Between all the parts of creation there is a beautiful consistency and a mutual relationship which shows that as the Author of the universe is infinite in knowledge and power, so He is *One*.

As to the existence of evil, moral and natural, it can

be accounted for by the liberty of action with which man and other moral agents were endowed, which liberty is essential to a system in which creatures render a voluntary obedience to their Creator. If there had been no possibility of sinning, there could have been no such thing as virtue, or moral excellence.

But again, what is often called *evil* arises necessarily from the limited nature of creatures, especially when the plan includes a scale of being, descending from the highest to the lowest. Every species, as you descend, is less perfect than those above it. Such a gradation involves necessarily the evil of partial defect. But properly speaking, this is no evil. Everything in the universe is good in its kind; but there is no absolute perfection but in God alone—none is good but God [*cf.* Matt. 19:17; Mark 10:18].

We do not assert that the argument for the unity of God from reason is absolutely demonstrative; it might be alleged that two or more beings, wise, powerful, and good, might be united in counsel, in the plan of the universe and the works of creation, just as several men might agree upon a plan of a temple or other building; and all the appearances would be the same, as if only one person were concerned. Let this be granted, and yet we may assert that reason cannot furnish the shadow of an argument in favor of a plurality of Gods. As far as she sees and speaks, her voice is in favor of the divine unity.

We feel less concerned to insist on anything further as evident from the light of nature, because the doctrine is clearly revealed and repeatedly taught in the Sacred Scriptures. All that we deem important to establish on this point is that reason teaches nothing contrary to the unity of God, and so far as she sheds any light on the subject, it is altogether in favor of the doctrine.

Let us then attend to the clear, unequivocal declarations of the Bible. "Hear, O Israel: The LORD our God is one LORD" (Deut. 6:4). "The Lord he is God; there is none else beside him" (Deut. 4:35). "Thou art the God, even thou alone of all the kingdoms of the earth" (2 Kings 19:15). "Thou, even thou, art Lord alone" (Neh. 9:6). "Thus saith the LORD the King of Israel, and his Redeemer the LORD of hosts; I am the first, and I am the last; and beside me there is no God" (Isa. 44:6). "Is there a God beside me? yea, there is no God; I know not any" (Isa. 44:8). "And this is life eternal, that they might know thee the only true God" (John 17:3). "But to us there is but one God" (1 Cor. 8:6). "God is one" (Gal. 3:20). "Thou believest that there is one God; thou doest well" (James 2:19).

It would be easy to multiply texts in confirmation of this doctrine, but these are sufficient. Indeed, no one who admits the Bible as authority can doubt on this subject; consequently, Jews and Christians have received the unity of God as a fundamental truth.

CHAPTER 5

Spirituality and Simplicity of the Divine Nature

Reason, as well as Scripture, requires us to believe that God is a pure Spirit. As God is an intelligent being, and the source of all intelligence, He must be a spirit; and as He is a voluntary agent, He must be an intelligent person. Matter is inert, unconscious, and cannot be the subject of thought or volition. Matter is also divisible to an indefinite extent and the parts of bodies are separate from each other, so that each particle is a separate existence. But unity belongs to mind, therefore the mind cannot be material. Again, all matter is solid and extended, and necessarily excludes all other bodies from occupying the same space; if then God were a material being, as He is omnipresent, He would exclude all other bodies from the universe. If He is not everywhere present, there would be some places where there was no God; and if limited to a certain locality, however extended it might be, there would be infinite space, in which God does not exist.

But if the materialist denies that inactivity, solidity, divisibility and extension are the natural properties of matter, and maintains that all matter consists of monads, which are in their nature active, indivisible, unextended, and that some of these, if not the whole, are endued with consciousness, and are susceptible of all the actions which we ascribe to mind, then there is no such thing as matter in the universe. Then everything that exists must fall under the class of spiritual being; for that substance which is active, indivisible, unextended, and capable of consciousness and other mental acts, is mind or spirit, and we cannot give a better definition of spirit than to deny to it those properties commonly ascribed to matter, and allowing to it the capacity of thought.

Materialists, therefore, in attempting to overthrow the belief of spiritual being, do in fact subvert the doctrine of the existence of matter, by affirming that it does not possess the properties commonly attributed to it, and does possess the powers and capabilities of spiritual existence. On this theory, the materialist becomes an immaterialist; and when men agree in the properties which belong to any substance, it matters little what name they give it. We leave the atheistical materialist to settle his account with natural philosophers, as to the properties of matter; and according to his own theory, all our arguments derived from the immateriality of the soul, for its incorruptibility or continued existence, stand in full force.

As God is a pure intelligence, and everywhere present, and everywhere active, He is a *Spirit*. Some, however, while they admitted this, held that God was the soul of the world, and that the world was to Him what our bodies are to us. This is one form of the doctrine of pantheism, which has been revived in our day. It is a monstrous notion to consider all bodies a part of the Supreme Being. It destroys all individuality and all accountability, and therefore, contradicts some of the clearest intuitions of our minds. Every man is conscious that he is a person, distinct from all other persons; and every man feels that he is capable of acting freely, and of doing good or evil, as a moral agent; and that he is accountable for his actions. All theories and reasonings which contradict self-evident principles of truth must be false and deserve no further consideration.

The Holy Scriptures everywhere represent God as a being of infinite intelligence, as a being of will and affection, as omnipotent and ever active, for all things are not only created but are upheld in being by His sustaining hand. Even active beings require His conservative energy to support them in being, and to continue their faculties in existence. Therefore, it is not only said that He upholdeth all things by His power, but that it is "in him we live, and move, and have our being" [Acts 17:28].

The Holy Scriptures enter into no nice disquisitions respecting matter and spirit, their properties and differences, but assume as true those first truths which are known without philosophy to every man of common sense.

That man is a free and accountable agent is not proved everywhere in the Bible, but is assumed as true and as well known as it can be. The same is true in regard to our nature consisting of soul and body, of which every man, who has his reason, is as well convinced as he could be by any revelation.

As soon as we know that there is a God, we feel constrained to admit that He must possess all excellence and every possible perfection, as stated before. And, therefore, as spirit is the most excellent kind of substance, and as God is made known to us as wise and powerful by creation, we cannot but believe that He is a pure spirit, uncompounded, and free from bodily parts and members. When God is spoken of as having head, hands, face, arms, feet, etc., it is necessary to consider this mode of speech as figurative, and intended to represent those things in the divine character or actions which bear some distant resemblance to what is found in man. Indeed, when God is said to be a Spirit, it is not to be understood that His essence, which is eternal and immutable, is of the same nature with created spirits, but only that there is a resemblance. If there were any substance known to us of a nobler nature than spirit, we should of course ascribe that to God, but still with the qualification that the essence of God is infinitely superior to all creatures. We need not be surprised, therefore, to find that there is but one text which positively asserts that God is a Spirit, excepting those which relate to the third person of the adorable Trinity; for this truth is everywhere assumed as known, and as implied in all His attributes. The text referred to is in John 4:24: "God is a Spirit: and they that worship him must worship him in spirit and in truth."

CHAPTER 6

Character of God

God is the maker of all things. He is therefore almighty. He is also wise. Of this our own body is sufficient enough. We are fearfully and wonderfully made [Ps. 139:14]. Our eyes and ears, our hands and feet, our mouths and stomach, our heart and blood-vessels, all attest the wisdom of God. We see it also in the inferior animals. Their bodies are formed with as much wisdom as our own. Every creature has a form, nature, appetites, and instincts suited to its condition in the world. The birds with their feathers and wings, the fishes with their fins, and the beasts with their feet of various kinds, are proofs of the wisdom of God. The trees, the flowers, and the grass do also show forth the wisdom of Him who gave them being. If we admire the wisdom of man in a watch, a telescope, or a steam engine, much more should we be filled with adoring wonder when we contemplate the infinitely superior wisdom of God displayed in all His works. Wherever we turn our eyes, we are met with the marks of wise design. The sun, which gives us light by day, and diffuses life through all nature, is a wonderful object. The moon and stars are beautiful and glorious works of the great Creator. Day and night, winter and summer, seed time and harvest, speak the wisdom of God. Indeed, the evidences of divine wisdom in everything

within us and around us are so innumerable, that it is
impossible to recount them.

We may, then, exclaim every hour, with the royal
Psalmist, "How manifold are thy works! in wisdom
hast thou made them all: the earth is full of thy riches"
[Ps. 104:24], or with the wise man, "The Lord by wisdom hath founded the earth; by understanding hath he
established the heavens" [Prov. 3:19], or with the prophet, "He hath made the earth by his power, he hath
established the world by his wisdom, and hath stretched
out the heavens by his discretion" [Jer. 10:12].

God is good. His goodness is manifest in every work
of His wisdom, for He hath so continued and arranged
all things in the best manner, to promote the happiness
of His creatures, according to their nature and capacity. Especially, His goodness appears in the capacity of
pleasure given to man, all the exercises and operations
of whose nature give him pleasure when indulged in
their proper measure. Man is formed with such a nature that he cannot open his eyes on the beautiful
world which he inhabits, without pleasure. The glory
of the firmament, the beauty of the landscape, and the
sublimity of the lofty mountains and vast ocean fill the
rational mind with pure delight. The various works of
nature or of art, perceived by the eye or ear, furnish a
feast to the mind. The food which nourishes us is pleasant to the taste and the water which gushes from the
earth affords a sweet refreshment. The light is pleasant to the eyes and the air is felt to be invigorating to
the lungs. Action is pleasant and so is repose. Sleep,
though it is the image of death, is sweet and refreshing
to the laboring man.

There are to man thousands of sources of pleasure.

If he were only innocent, even the world as it is, though laboring under a curse for sin, would still furnish many of the delights of paradise. Truly, God is good. To Moses He said, "I will make all my goodness to pass before thee" [Exod. 33:19]. And when He proclaimed to His servant His name, a part of it was, "abundant in goodness and truth" [Exod. 34:6]. "The earth is full of the goodness of the Lord" [Ps. 33:5]. O how great is thy goodness, which thou hast laid up for them that fear thee! "The goodness of God endureth continually" [Ps. 52:1].

God is holy. Every excellence is His, and without holiness He would not be an object of veneration. The dictates of our own conscience teach us that the Father of our spirits is holy. No attribute of Jehovah is more clearly and frequently brought to view in the Bible. Holiness is the true ground of that adoration which enters so essentially into the worship of God. "Worship at his footstool; for he is holy" [Ps. 99:5]. "But thou art holy, thou that inhabitest the praises of Israel" [Ps. 22:3]. "The Lord is holy in all his works" [Ps. 145:17]. Holiness is the sum of all moral excellence. When the heavenly hosts worship Jehovah, they ascribe holiness to Him in the most emphatic manner: "Holy, Holy, Holy, is the Lord of Hosts" [Isa. 6:3]. And the four symbolical living creatures whom John saw before the throne of the Most High, "rest not day and night, saying, Holy, Holy, Holy, Lord God Almighty, which was, and is, and is to come" [Rev. 4:8]. Everything which has any relation to God, or His worship, is holy; His word, His house, His angels, His prophets, His people, His sabbaths, and all the places where He records His name, and all the institutions by which He is worshipped. "There is none holy as the Lord" [1 Sam. 2:2].

God is also just and righteous, giving to every one his due. Justice is the rectitude of God's nature. Justice is essential to Him as governor of the world. "Shall not the Judge of all the earth do right?" [Gen. 18:25]. "Justice and judgment are the habitation of thy throne" [Ps. 89:14]. "The Lord is righteous in all his ways, and holy in all his works" [Ps. 145:17]. "He will by no means spare the guilty" [*cf.* Exod. 34:7; Num. 14:18]. The Lord is the righteous Judge. "And I heard the angel say, Thou art righteous, O Lord" [Rev. 16:5]. "True and righteous are thy judgments" [Rev. 16:7].

God is great. "The Lord is a great God" [Ps. 95:3]. "Thou art great, O Lord God, none is like unto thee" [*cf.* Jer. 10:6]. When Solomon was engaged in erecting the temple, he said, "The house which I build is great, for great is our God" [2 Chron. 2:5]. Thus also Nehemiah, in his prayer, calls God, "The great, the mighty, and the terrible God" (Neh. 9:32). And Isaiah, "Great is the Holy One of Israel in the midst of thee" (Isa. 12:6). And Jeremiah, "Thou art great, and thy name is great in might" (Jer. 10:6). Mention is often made in Scripture of God's "great name." "What wilt thou do unto thy great name" (Josh. 7:9)? "Behold, I have sworn by my great name" (Jer. 44:9). "Thou art great, and thy name is great" (Jer. 10:6). "My name shall be great among the Gentiles" [Mal. 1:11]. By the "name" of God we should understand His attributes. God is great in all his perfections; and "his greatness is unsearchable" [Ps. 145:3].

God is eternal. He has had no beginning, and He will have no end. This perpetuity of existence is frequently expressed in the Bible, by saying, He is, and was, and is to come. Of His years there is no end: "Before the mountains were brought forth," said Moses, "or ever thou hadst formed the earth or the world, even from everlasting to everlasting, thou art God" [Ps. 90:2]. Eternity is often ascribed to God in Scripture. "Unto the King eternal" [1 Tim. 1:17]. "The eternal God is thy refuge" [Deut. 33:27]. "His eternal power and Godhead" [Rom. 1:20]. Indeed, the idea of eternity, though incomprehensible, forces itself upon us when we think of the First Cause. He who is the Creator of all things can have no beginning. To suppose the contrary would involve us in the grossest absurdity.

As God is eternal, so He is unchangeable. He says of himself, "I change not" [Mal. 3:6]. He is the Father of lights, with whom "there is no variableness, neither shadow of turning" [James 1:17]. His purposes and plans are as unchangeable as His nature. "My counsel shall stand, and I will do all my pleasure" [Isa. 46:10]. Any change in the essence or will of Jehovah would argue weakness, or want of perfect knowledge of all contingencies.

God knows all things. "Thou God seest me" [Gen. 16:13]. "The Lord searcheth the hearts and trieth the reins of the children of men" [*cf.* Rev. 2:23]. There is nothing hidden from His sight. All things are naked and open before him with whom we have to do [Heb. 4:13]. He seeth "the end from the beginning" [*cf.* Isa. 46:10]. All the free actions of His creatures are known to Him, for He hath most exactly foretold many such actions, as is evident from His predictions respecting the treachery of Judas, the denial of Peter, and the

malice and envy of His crucifiers. If the Lord was not
omniscient, He could not possibly govern the world with
wisdom. But no truth is more clearly revealed, and no
attribute is more essential to the perfection of Jehovah.
"For thou, even thou only knowest the hearts of all the
children of men" [1 Kings 8:39; 2 Chron. 6:30].

God is everywhere. "Am I a God at hand, saith the
Lord, and not a God afar off?" [Jer. 23:23]. "If I ascend
up into heaven, thou art there; if I make my bed in
hell, behold thou art there. If I take the wings of the
morning and dwell in the uttermost parts of the sea,
even there shall thy hand lead me, and thy right hand
shall hold me" [Ps. 139:9-10]. "For his eyes are on the
ways of man, and he seeth all his goings" [Job 34:21].
"Behold, I fill heaven and earth" [Jer. 23:24]. And yet
the heaven of heavens cannot contain Him. And He is
not only present, but active. He sustains all things by
the word of His power. He is the living God. "In him
we live and move and have our being" [Acts 17:28].

God is incomprehensible. "Canst thou by searching
find out God? canst thou find out the Almighty unto
perfection?" [Job 11:7]. "Such knowledge is too wonderful for me; it is high, I cannot attain to it" [Ps. 139:6].
His greatness is unsearchable. "There is no searching of
his understanding" [Isa. 40:28]. "O the depth of the
riches both of the wisdom and knowledge of God; how
unsearchable are his judgments, and his ways past
finding out" [Rom. 11:33]. "Lo these are parts of his
ways: but how little a portion is heard of Him? but the
thunder of his power who can understand?" [Job 26:14].
And so it will ever be, for the time can never come when
the finite shall comprehend the infinite. Hereafter,
much of the darkness which now overspreads the divine

character and dispensations, will be dissipated. New mysteries will be forever rising to the view of the contemplative mind! But if we have all the knowledge of God, of which our finite minds are susceptible, we should desire no more. An increasing knowledge of God will be one of the chief felicities of heaven.

God is merciful and gracious. Unless this attribute of mercy had been clearly revealed, a knowledge of all other attributes would give us little comfort. Even the goodness of God would hold out no consolation to sinners, who had forfeited every claim to divine benefits. When inexorable justice holds criminals in its grasp, of what account is it to them that their king dispenses favors to his obedient subjects? Man, by nature, is justly condemned. Justice cannot be set aside; it must have its demand, or God must change. Then the only relief is the mercy and grace of God. Mercy can only have room for exercise when justice is satisfied. And this wonderful work has been accomplished by the atonement of the Son of God. "God so loved the world that he gave his only begotten son, that whosoever believeth in him should not perish, but have everlasting life" [John 3:16]. "Not that we loved God, but that he loved us, and sent his Son to be the propitiation for our sins" [1 John 4:10].

The chief object of divine revelation was to reveal the mercy of God. That God was good and would do good to His obedient creatures reason could teach; and that He was just and would render to every one his due was also a dictate of natural religion. But how God could be just and justify the ungodly was a problem which human reason could never solve. That, however, which is impossible to man is possible with God.

"Mercy and truth are met together; righteousness and peace have kissed each other" [Ps. 85:10]. Through the satisfaction made by Christ's atonement to divine justice, the door of mercy has been opened and a free salvation offered to the guilty.

The love of God to sinners, which is the same as His mercy, is much spoken of in the Word of God. And indeed it is, at once, the most delightful and wonderful object which can engage the contemplation of any human being. This love has its origin in the divine mind; there was nothing in the character of fallen man to excite it. It is, therefore, sovereign, free, and from everlasting. The depth and height and length and breadth of this love pass all knowledge. The bright evidence of its strength and freeness is found in the gift of His only begotten Son. "The Lord is merciful and gracious, slow to anger and plenteous in mercy" [Ps. 103:8]. "As the heaven is high above the earth, so great is his mercy toward them that fear him" [Ps. 103:11]. When He proclaimed His name to Moses, it was, "The Lord God, merciful and gracious, longsuffering and abundant in goodness and truth, keeping mercy for thousands, forgiving iniquity and transgression and sin" [Exod. 34:6-7]. The songs of praise addressed to God in the ancient church were often concluded with the chorus, "The mercy of the Lord endureth forever." "O give thanks unto the Lord, for his mercy endureth forever." "Let Israel now say, that his mercy endureth forever."

God is a God of truth and faithfulness. Truth is His very nature. All His declarations are true. "Thy word is truth" [John 17:17]. And as He has consented to enter into covenants with men, and to make great and precious promises to His people, He is faithful in fulfilling whatever He has spoken. No part of the good which He has ever promised has failed or ever can fail of its accomplishment. "And ye know in all your hearts, and in all your souls, that not one thing hath failed of all the good things which the Lord your God spake concerning you" [Josh. 23:14]. "Know therefore that the Lord thy God, he is God, the faithful God, which keepeth covenant and mercy with them that love him and keep his commandments to a thousand generations" [Deut. 7:9]. He is therefore styled the "covenant-keeping God" [Dan. 9:4].

As He is faithful in the fulfillment of His promises, so is He true in the execution of His threatenings against impenitent transgressors. To suppose that His denunciations of vengeance against sinners were merely spoken to produce terror is most dishonoring to the God of truth. "The strength of Israel will not lie" [1 Sam. 15:29]. "God is not a man that he should lie" [Num. 23:19]. "Hath he spoken, and shall he not make it good?" "Surely thou wilt slay the wicked, O God" [Ps. 139:19]. "The Lord will take vengeance on his adversaries, and he reserveth wrath for his enemies" [Nah. 1:2]. If in any case His threatenings are not executed, it is because a condition was implied, as when God threatens an individual or a nation with destruction, and that individual or nation takes warning and repents, then His wrath is turned away. In all such threats there is an implied condition, that if the guilty will repent, they shall escape the threatened destruction. Indeed, the very end of addressing such threatenings to men is to bring them to repentance, that they may escape condign punishment.

God is longsuffering and forbearing toward the

children of men. "He is not slack concerning his promise, as some men count slackness, but is longsuffering to usward, not willing that any should perish, but that all should come to repentance" [2 Pet. 3:9]. He endureth "with much longsuffering the vessels of wrath fitted to destruction" [Rom. 9:22]. This forbearance of the Almighty is often abused by wicked men. "Because judgment is not speedily executed against an evil work, therefore the heart of the children of men is fully set in them to do evil" [Eccles. 8:11].

God condescends and is compassionate. When we consider the majesty of God, nothing is more wonderful than His condescension. "He humbleth himself to behold the things that are in heaven, and in the earth" [Ps. 113:6]. "What is man that thou art mindful of him? or the son of man that thou visitest him?" [Ps. 8:4; Heb. 2:6]. Though the Lord be high yet hath he respect unto the lowly" [Ps. 138:6]. "Though heaven be his throne and earth his footstool, yet to this man will he look who is of an humble and contrite spirit and trembleth at his word" [cf. Isa. 66:1-1; Isa. 57:15]. "Like as a father pitieth his children, so the Lord pitieth them that fear him" [Ps. 103:13].

God is supreme. "His kingdom ruleth over all and he doth according to his will, in the armies of heaven and among the inhabitants of the earth" [Dan. 4:35]. All honor, glory, blessing, and praise should be ascribed to God.

CHAPTER 7

The Holy Trinity

The scriptural evidence of this doctrine would not be deemed insufficient by anyone were it not for the idea that there is something in the doctrine repugnant to reason; or, which it is very difficult to reconcile to right reason. The only thing that reason has to do with the subject is to examine whether there is anything in the orthodox doctrine of the Trinity which is manifestly repugnant to any truth clearly ascertained by the use of right reason. It is admitted that this doctrine is not known by the light of nature; for even if there should be found in the material universe or in the human mind, a resemblance to the Trinity, as some have supposed, this resemblance, if admitted, would furnish no conclusive argument in favor of the doctrine. It is not pretended that the doctrine is either made known or can be proved by reasoning. It is a doctrine of pure revelation. But if its opponents could show that it contradicted any clear and universally acknowledged principles of truth, we should be reduced to the necessity of either rejecting the Bible, which teaches the doctrine, or of so interpreting the Scriptures, as to exclude the absurd opinion. The first course is pursued by deists, who often give as a sufficient reason for rejecting the Bible that it contains doctrines contrary to reason. Jews and Mohammedans are found making the same objection. But all anti-trinitarian Christians adopt the second course. They admit the evidences of divine revelation to be convincing, and they therefore receive the Scriptures as a true revelation. But as they think that this doctrine is contrary to reason, they determine that it cannot be the doctrine of divine revelation; and in consequence, exert all their force to destroy the authority of such texts as seem to contain it, or so interpret them that they may speak a different language.

It seems necessary, therefore, to inquire whether, indeed, there is anything in the doctrine of the Trinity palpably contradictory, or evidently incompatible with evident principles of reason. Here it is important to distinguish between doctrines which are above reason and those which are contrary to reason. That many things which are certainly true are above reason must be admitted by every rational man that will consider the subject. That God is without beginning is as certain a truth as any which could be mentioned, and yet it is above reason. Who can comprehend a duration without a beginning? And from this incomprehensible truth, even atheism would give no relief; for the atheist is obliged to admit that something has existed from eternity, unless he choose to say that all existing things originated without cause, which would be still more incomprehensible. That God is everywhere present is admitted by Unitarians; and yet they must maintain that there can be no diffusion of the divine essence through the parts of space; but that the whole Deity is everywhere. Is not this above reason? And who can comprehend the divine omniscience? Indeed, as all the attributes of God are infinite, that very term shows that they transcend human reason; for no finite mind can comprehend that which is infinite. There are also facts which relate to our own existence, the truth of which we know certainly, and yet we are utterly unable to comprehend them. Who can explain the true cause of muscular motion in the human body?

Nothing is more certain in our experience than that our minds and bodies are intimately united, so that they constantly and reciprocally affect each other. How it is that we perceive by the eye, hear by the ear, distinguish tastes by the tongue, or odors by the smell, are all mysteries. They are truths, but they are above reason. Now it is readily admitted that the doctrine of a Trinity, in the divine essence, falls into the class of incomprehensible truths. We know it to be a truth because God, who cannot lie, has plainly declared it; but *how* it is, or how it can be, is above our comprehension, just as some of the fundamental truths of natural religion, which have been mentioned, are above reason.

It is alleged, however, that God's being at the same time one and three is plainly repugnant to reason, the proposition containing a palpable contradiction. This statement Trinitarians utterly deny, and certainly the external evidence is very much against it; for much the greater number of wise and impartial men, who have carefully examined the subject since Christianity was introduced, have believed in the doctrine of the Trinity. But let us examine this objection and see whether it has any foundation. If Trinitarians asserted that the persons of the Trinity were three and one, in the same sense, there would indeed be an evident contradiction; but this is so far from being the fact that all writers on the subject are careful to state that while there are three distinctions, called *persons*, there is but one essence. But it is alleged that if there be three *persons*, there must be three Gods; for a *person* is a distinct, intelligent, and voluntary agent; and if there be three distinct, intelligent, voluntary agents, there must be three Gods. But who can show it to involve any contradiction that three equal intelligences should be united in the possession of a common essence?

The whole force of this objection arises from taking the word *person* in a strict and definite sense, as used when applied to men; whereas, we are under no necessity of retaining this word; it is not found in Scripture, and many Trinitarians have rejected it. There may be three in the divine essence, and yet these may not with much propriety be called persons. Still, in our opinion, there is no need to depart from the terms commonly made use of by Trinitarians. Some term is necessary to designate the three, and there is no objection to the word *person*, which would not exist in full force against any other word; and this term has the sanction of long usage, and is found in almost every writer on the subject. All that is necessary is, as in analogous cases, to explain the sense in which the word is used in application to the Father, Son, and Holy Spirit.

Here it should be remembered that all our language which we use to designate the attributes of God is necessarily inadequate; and the most common words in application to the Deity have a peculiar meaning. This is the fact when we use the words intellect, will, purpose, love, etc. God's understanding is infinitely different from ours; the will of God cannot be understood as precisely similar to will in the human mind. And in regard to affections and passions this is so evident, that many, to avoid the ascription of any imperfection to the

Supreme Being, have denied to Him every kind of affection as well as passion. In the use of such terms, it should be considered that they must not be taken definitely and strictly, as they apply to man, but as representing vaguely and indefinitely something in God which resembles those things in man for which these words stand. And no other rule, in the use of the term *person*, is necessary, when the word is used in relation to the Supreme Being, than what is necessary in many other cases. The word *person* is used merely to mark a distinction evidently made in Scripture and may, in this indefinite sense, be properly used; because, in relation to Father, Son, and Spirit, personal pronouns are used and personal acts are ascribed to them.

The question respecting the truth of the Trinity is, however, not to be confounded with the one respecting the propriety of the use of the word *persons*, which some who hold the doctrine of the Trinity firmly, have rejected. And some, who nevertheless believed in the Father, Son, and Holy Spirit, as being divine, have scrupled to use the word Trinity, because it is not found in Holy Scripture. Now, while men receive implicitly all that is taught in Scripture respecting each of these, we need not contend with them about the theological terms which shall be employed.

Though the Trinity is not a doctrine discoverable by reason, yet we find some vestiges of it in nearly all ancient systems of pagan theology, which seems to indicate that it was handed down by tradition from the earliest ages of the world. But we do not adduce this as a fact likely to have any weight with the anti-trinitarian. Indeed, some have ingeniously founded an argument against the doctrine from its resemblance to

Platonism and other pagan systems. But still, no more reasonable account of the triad, found in most ancient theories of religion, can be given, than by supposing an early tradition to have been received on this subject. Our appeal, however, must be to the infallible oracles of divine revelation; and although we find many vestiges of a plurality of persons in the Godhead in the Old Testament, yet as these are not so evident but that they are liable to dispute, it will save time to proceed at once to the testimonies which are found in the New Testament. And our first object will be to show that three persons are often mentioned together by three distinct names, and then we will bring convincing arguments to prove that each of these is God. There being but one God, as we have seen, these three must, in some mysterious way, be united in one essence.

At the baptism of Christ, the Father spake from heaven, saying, "This is my beloved son, in whom I am well pleased" [Matt. 3:17; Mark 1:11], and the Holy Ghost descended on Christ in the form of a dove. Here then we have Christ visible in the form of man, the Father speaking of the Son in a voice from heaven, and the Holy Ghost, in a visible form, descending on Christ. Whatever may be determined respecting the nature of these persons, they are manifestly three in number. The Holy Ghost did not speak, and the Father did speak, but did not descend in a visible form; and, evidently, the Son was not the person who spoke or descended. This evident manifestation of three persons at the baptism of Christ, led one of the Christian fathers to exclaim, "Let him who would have a proof of the Trinity go to Jordan."

The clear distinction of the persons of the Father,

Son, and Holy Spirit, is again most evidently set forth in Christ's consolatory discourse to His disciples before He suffered, recorded in John 14-16, and also in His intercessory prayer of John 17. "And I will pray the Father, and he shall give you another Comforter, that shall abide with you forever; even the Spirit of truth, whom the world cannot receive, because it seeth him not, neither knoweth him; but ye know him, for he dwelleth with you, and shall be in you" [John 14:16-17]. Here the Son prays to the Father for the Comforter, the Spirit. That there are three mentioned is too evident to need proof.

Another clear testimony to the truth that there are three distinct persons in the divine essence is found in the form of Christian baptism, which Christ gave to His apostles in the commission which He gave them just before His ascension to heaven. "Go," said He, "teach all nations, baptizing them in the name of the Father, and of the Son, and of the Holy Ghost" [Matt. 28:19]. These are among the most solemn and important words in the New Testament; they contain the commission under which not only the apostles, but all ministers of the gospel act, and the form of words directed to be used in baptism was intended to be employed in the administration of this ordinance through all periods of the church. All persons who have ever been regularly baptized have had these words pronounced over them, while emblematically or sacramentally washed from their sins. Into whose name then have all Christians, from the beginning, been baptized? Into the name of the Father, of the Son, and of the Holy Ghost. Undoubtedly, Christians are baptized into the name of God; but God is here represented as three. It would indeed be incredible that baptism should be in the name of the Supreme God, of a man or mere creature, and of a divine attribute. The mention of such an interpretation is enough to refute it. Undoubtedly our Lord, in His commission, must have intended by Father, Son, and Holy Ghost, to designate three persons. Whether they are all to be considered as partaking of the divine nature is not now the immediate object of inquiry, but whether three persons are designated. The divinity of each will be hereafter proved.

Again, the apostolical benediction, recorded in 2 Corinthians 13:14, is another conclusive evidence of the existence of three persons in the Godhead: "The grace of the Lord Jesus Christ, and the love of God, and the communion of the Holy Ghost, be with you all. Amen." Here grace is implored of the Son, love from God the Father, and communion from the Holy Ghost. It is impossible, by any proper rules of interpretation, to evade the conclusion that three divine persons are here named. Similar proof we have in Ephesians 2:18: "For through him (Christ) we both have access by one Spirit unto the Father." Here the same three persons are brought into view, and designated by their appropriate appellatives. Another passage in which the three persons are distinctly mentioned together is 1 Peter 1:2, which says, "Elect according to the foreknowledge of God the Father, through sanctification of the Spirit, unto obedience and sprinkling of the blood of Jesus Christ." Here again, we find the same three persons clearly distinguished.

Although the text in 1 John 5:7 has been disputed on plausible grounds, and the testimony of existing manuscripts is unfavorable to its authenticity, yet there being positive evidence that ancient manuscripts which contained it have been destroyed or lost, I think it should not be omitted in a summary of the evidence of the doctrine of the Trinity, as I have a strong persuasion that it is really a precious part of inspired Scripture which we are not at liberty to abandon, but which was probably insidiously dropped out of the copies in the days of Arian ascendency. What confirms me in this opinion is that it is evidently referred to both by Tertullian and Cyprian, who lived long before our oldest extant manuscripts were written. The words are, "There are three that bear record in heaven, the Father, the Word, and the Holy Ghost, and these three are one." Here we have our whole doctrine expressed, as clearly as it could be done in words.

The evidence of three distinct persons has now, we think, been established beyond all reasonable contradiction, as the doctrine clearly and repeatedly inculcated in the Scriptures of truth.

CHAPTER 8

Divinity of Christ

The proof of the deity of the Son of God is the main point in establishing the doctrine of the Trinity; for if it can be clearly shown that there is a second person in the divine essence, there will be small repugnance to the admission of a third.

Here it may be observed that the appellation "Son of God" is remarkable. A son is always of the same nature with the father who begat him and possesses the same attributes. It is true that Adam, in Luke's genealogy of Christ, is called the son of God, by which no more is to be understood but that God was his immediate Creator. But Christ is called not only *the Son of God*, but His *"only begotten son"* (John 1:14). And angels are called "sons of God" [Job 1:6; Job 2:1], as being immediately created by Him; but the apostle Paul distinguishes the sonship of Christ from that of angels in that remarkable passage in Heb 1:5-8, where he says, "For unto which of the angels said he at any time, thou art my Son, this day have I begotten thee? And again, I will be to him a Father, and he shall be to me a Son? And again, when he bringeth in the first-begotten into the world, he saith, And let all the angels of God worship him. And of the angels he saith, Who maketh his angels spirits, and his ministers a flame of fire. But unto the Son he saith, Thy throne, O God, is forever and ever" [Heb. 1:7-8].

Here we learn that the Son is not one of the angels, for He is clearly distinguished from them all. Not only so, but the angels were commanded to worship Him, when He made His first appearance in the world. Now He whom angels worship can be no other than God. Was it ever heard of, or anywhere read, that the angels were commanded to worship one another? No, but they did receive a command to worship the Son. This shows that Christ was not called Son merely on account of His miraculous birth, or His designation to office as Mediator, or His resurrection from the dead. All these may serve to show that He is the Son of God, but He was Son from the beginning—by nature a Son—eternally begotten; for as Son, He is to be worshipped by the most exalted angels of heaven. And while He is addressed by the Father as a Son, He is emphatically addressed as God: "Thy throne, O God, is forever and ever" [Heb. 1:8]. To which of the angels was ever an address like this made? As these words are a quotation from Psalm 45:6, by turning to the passage we find that the person addressed is called *the King*, and is addressed as the *Most Mighty*.

There is, moreover, another argument for the eternity of Christ contained in this pregnant passage, which is of the most conclusive nature. Indeed, it is so cogent that this being impartially weighed, all further arguments seem to be superfluous. It is derived from the fact plainly declared by the apostle, and made prominent in several other parts of Scripture, that Christ, here called the Son of God, is the *Creator* of the universe. Surely He who created all things must be God, or all distinction between God and the creature is obliterated. How do we know that there is a God but by the creation? The idea that the power of creation may be delegated to a creature is to suppose that a creature may be rendered omnipotent and infinitely wise; that is, that a creature may be endowed with divine attributes, or that there may be another God.

The notion that Christ was employed in creation as an instrument, is still less reasonable, for as creation is an instantaneous work of almighty power, what place was there for any instrumentality? Besides, in the passage under consideration there is no allusion to any instrument. It is simply and plainly declared, "Thou, Lord, in the beginning, hast laid the foundation of the earth, and the heavens are the work of thy hands" [Heb. 1:10]. In the second verse, it is indeed said, "By whom he made all the worlds" [Heb. 1:2], but in the order of operation in the persons of the Trinity, the Son is always represented as acting in conformity with the will of the Father, but still as exercising the same power, and possessing the same knowledge. The very name "Father" indicates that He is primary in order of existence and of operation; by some, therefore, He has been called the fountain of the Deity. Thus our Lord says, "For as the Father hath life in himself, so hath he given to the Son to have life in himself" [John 5:26]. "All things are delivered to me of my Father, and no man knoweth the Son but the Father, neither knoweth any man the Father save the Son, and he to whomsoever the Son will reveal him" [Matt. 11:27]. Here the knowledge of the Father by the Son is put on a level with the knowledge which the Father has of the Son; and the nature of the Son is represented as incomprehensible to all others but the Father, just as the nature of the Father is incomprehensible to all but the Son. An equality in the possession of divine attributes is here as clearly taught as is possible. Can it be a mere creature who knows the essence of God, as his essence is known by God? That is impossible.

But let us attend more particularly to the argument from the creation of the heavens and the earth, and all which they contain. There are several other testimonies to this fact which it may be expedient to bring into view. In John 1:3, Christ, under the name *Logos*, is not only said to have been in the beginning *with* God, but to *be* God; and the evangelist goes on to say, "All things were made by him, and without him was not any thing made that was made" [John 1:3]. He is also declared to be the source of life and of light. "In him was life, and the life was the light of men" [John 1:4]; "That was the true light that lighteth every man that cometh into the world" [John 1:9]. And that there might be no doubt respecting the person denominated *Logos*, it is said, "And the Word (*Logos*) was made flesh, and dwelt among us, (and we beheld his glory, the glory as of the only begotten of the Father,) full of grace and truth" [John 1:14].

It is reported by some of the earliest of the Christian fathers that John wrote his gospel for the very purpose of refuting the errors of certain heretics who denied the divinity of the Son. And whether that was the occasion of his writing or not, he could not have asserted the doctrine more clearly and explicitly than he has done. And how do anti-trinitarians evade the force of this passage? The Arians maintain that the Son performed the work of creation by a delegated power, or as an instrument. But this interpretation will not suit the Socinians and all who deny the existence of Christ before He was born of Mary. They, therefore, have invented a gloss, which certainly no common reader would ever have thought of, and which nothing but dire necessity could ever have induced anyone to adopt; namely that Christ was the author of the new dispensation, and disposed of and regulated everything in the Christian church. When men are driven to such forced interpretations, it is a clear evidence that they cannot maintain their ground by solid argument. It is a kind of *reductio ad absurdum*; and we should be satisfied to leave the matter there. There is no need of an elaborate refutation of that which so plainly refutes itself.

Another remarkable testimony to the fact that Christ is the creator of all things, is found in Colossians 1:15-17: "Who is the image of the invisible God, the firstborn of every creature. For by him were all things created, that are in heaven, and that are in earth, visible and invisible; whether they be thrones, or dominions, or principalities, or powers: all things were created by him and for him; and he is before all things, and by him all things consist."

Here, not only the creation of the visible universe is ascribed to the Son, but also all things invisible; and lest any should be disposed to confine this work to inanimate substances, the whole hierarchy of heaven is declared also to have been created by Him. The most exalted of the celestial host are His creatures. And not only so, but all things are continually supported by Him. The expression, "firstborn of every creature" [Col. 1:15], has misled many to think that this scripture asserted that Christ was the first formed creature;

but the most judicious critics have shown that this is not the proper meaning of the original term. The true sense is, "first begotten before all creation"; that is, from eternity. The same idea is expressed in the last verse cited, "and he is before all things." "From the foundation of the world"—"before the foundation of the world"—"before all things," are the modes of speech by which an eternity past is expressed in Scripture.

One would think that none could resort to the forced interpretation which has been put on the passage in John, but what else can the Unitarian do? He has no other refuge from the convincing force of the testimony, unless he should have recourse to the supposition that the whole passage is spurious; but there is no proof of any such thing. No text in the Bible is more certainly authentic. The Unitarian is therefore obliged, as before, to pretend that the apostle is not speaking of the creation of the world, but of the setting up the gospel kingdom. If absurdity were stamped on the face of this interpretation when applied to the passage in John, what shall we say of it here, where the heavens and the earth are expressly mentioned; and not only so, but things visible and invisible; and finally, the glorious hosts of heaven, angels, dominions, principalities and powers, are mentioned among His works. And all these He upholds by His power. Is there any passage in the Bible where the creation of all things is more expressly and particularly ascribed to the Father than here to the Son? To attempt to apply the language here used, in the midst of a plain didactic discourse, to the setting up of the Christian church, or introducing a new dispensation, is so unreasonable at first view that there is really no need of a refutation.

What could be meant by the heavens and the earth?
What could be meant by things visible and invisible, or
by the names of the celestial orders? If such an
interpretation could be admitted, then the testimonies
of the Holy Scriptures would be utterly useless. No text
on any subject could be brought forward in proof of the
unity, or of any of the attributes of God, which might
not be turned aside with as much show of reason as is
exhibited in this interpretation.

In the text in the gospel of John, they demurred,
because the word used for *made*, was not the one
commonly used to express a creation out of nothing,
but here we have the very word, used by the Seventy
[the Septuagint] to express the work of creation in
Genesis 1. In the former case, the objection had no
force, but in this there is no foundation for it. This wild
notion, by which, in the foregoing testimonies, they
would have us by the creation of all things in heaven
and earth to understand the setting up a new kingdom,
or introducing a new dispensation after the advent of
Christ, cannot possibly be applied to the text in Hebrews 1; for there it is declared that the heaven and
earth of which he spake, the creation of which he
ascribed to the Son of God, should perish—and that
they should wax old as doth a garment, and that as a
vesture they should be folded up and changed. But
surely this cannot apply to the kingdom of Christ, or
the new creation, for this is everlasting.

If there is a doctrine plainly taught in the Bible,
this is one, that Christ is the Creator of all things; and
if so, He must be truly God. We have no higher idea of
God than Creator of heaven and earth. If another
besides the true God may be the Creator, then another

besides God possesses those attributes by the manifestation of which in the works of nature we know that there is a God, and by which His almighty power and infinite wisdom are made known.

It seems unnecessary to adduce other arguments, as this is of itself as demonstrative of the deity of Christ as if we had a thousand. The mind which can resist this would resist any number. If it were necessary, we could adduce hundreds of texts in which the doctrine is expressed or implied. We shall, therefore, conclude by observing that Christ is called Jehovah— the great God, the mighty God, the true God. And arguments for His divinity might be derived from His miracles, as from His glorious work of redemption, as from the worship and obedience demanded, and from His being appointed the Judge of the quick and the dead—of angels and of men. But it is deemed unnecessary to deduce arguments from all these topics, as what has been said is sufficient.

CHAPTER 9

Personality of the Holy Spirit

The divinity of the Holy Spirit may be established by arguments of the same kind as have been adduced in support of the deity of the Son. It does not seem necessary to go over the same ground again, especially, as at present there are none, as far as we know, who maintain that the Holy Spirit is a created being. Antitrinitarians of the present day admit that the Spirit is divine, but not a distinct person from the Father. As the spirit of a man is the man himself, so they think that the Spirit of God is God, or the wisdom or power of God. Another reason why it is not necessary now to enter into an elaborate argument to establish the divinity of the Spirit is that reason makes no greater objection to a Trinity than a duality in the Godhead. If the proofs of the deity of the Son are conclusive, the same kind of evidence will readily be received in favor of a third person. We shall, therefore, occupy the space which can be allotted for this point to a consideration of the proofs of the distinct personality of the Holy Spirit. And here the reader will recollect the observations made respecting the sense in which the word *person* is used when applied to the divine essence. We do not pretend that we are able to form definite and clear conceptions on this subject. Among creatures, where we find an intelligent, voluntary agent, we call that being a person. Such persons are spoken of by proper names, and by personal pronouns, which are used instead of the name. For example, "John" is possessed of reason and will, and he pursues such objects as are agreeable to his taste. John is a person. Every one who is constituted like John, however he may differ from him in other respects, is also called a person.

We find in Scripture three to whom divine attributes and works are ascribed, each of whom has an appropriate name and is frequently represented as acting, feeling, and speaking; to each of these the pronouns used in reference to persons are often applied. They are not different names of the same person because they are, in a number of cases, all mentioned in the same sentence; they are represented as speaking to each other, and as sending or promising to send another. And there are appropriate acts ascribed to each. It cannot be supposed that if the Holy Spirit were not a distinct person, this mode of speaking of Him in the Holy Scriptures would be kept up whenever He is mentioned. Sometimes, by a lively figure, that which is not a person is personified, and introduced as thinking, feeling, seeing, hearing, and speaking, but no one is ever deceived by this liberty of speech. If this personification were kept up whenever this inanimate, unintelligent being was mentioned, it would tend only to confusion and error. But this is never done in regard to such beings as are not possessed of intelligence.

Let it then be kept distinctly in view that the Holy Spirit is either a person or a divine attribute, as none now are found maintaining that the Holy Spirit is a creature; and if He were, He would still be a person.

What we now wish to establish is the distinct personality of the Holy Spirit.

The personality of the Paraclete, who is the Holy Ghost, is exceedingly manifest from the words of Christ when He promises to pray the Father to send the Holy Spirit (John 14:16-17), where the personal pronoun is used to designate the Holy Ghost no less than six times in two verses. "And I will pray the Father, and he shall give you another Comforter, that he may abide with you forever: even the Spirit of truth, whom the world cannot receive, because it seeth him not, neither knoweth him: but ye know him; for he dwelleth with you, and shall be in you." And again, in John 14:26, "But the Comforter (Paraclete), which is the Holy Ghost, whom the Father will send in my name, he shall teach you all things," etc. Also, in John 16:7-14, "Nevertheless I tell you the truth; it is expedient for you that I go away; for if I go not away, the Comforter will not come unto you; but if I depart, I will send him unto you. And when he is come, he will reprove the world of sin, and of righteousness, and of judgment: of sin, because they believe not on me; of righteousness, because I go to my Father, and ye see me no more; of judgment, because the prince of this world is judged. I have yet many things to say unto you, but ye cannot bear them now. Howbeit, when he, the Spirit of truth, is come, he will guide you into all truth: for he shall not speak of himself; but whatsoever he shall hear, that shall he speak: and he will shew you things to come. He shall glorify me: for he shall receive of mine, and shall shew it unto you."

In this last passage, the personal pronoun is applied to the Holy Spirit nearly a dozen times. And there is a peculiar force in the original, which cannot be preserved in English. The Greek word for *Spirit* is of the neuter gender, but the inspired writer, instead of making use of a pronoun of the corresponding gender, constantly uses the pronoun of the masculine gender. No conceivable reason can be assigned for this, except that the Spirit is really a person, a divine person, and therefore should be represented by the masculine pronoun.

How would it sound to attribute to any divine attribute, or operation, what is ascribed to the Holy Spirit, throughout the Scriptures? "I will pray to the Father, and he will send his wisdom, and he shall teach you all things. He will not speak of himself, but he will take of mine and shew it unto you. And when wisdom is come, he will convince the world of sin, of righteousness, and judgment." "Why hath Satan filled thine heart to lie unto Wisdom?" "He that blasphemeth against Wisdom, it shall never be forgiven him, neither in this world, nor in that which is to come." "As Wisdom said by David." "Wisdom said, separate me Barnabas and Saul to the work to which I have appointed them." "I baptize you in the name of the Father, Son, and Wisdom." "The grace of our Lord Jesus Christ, the love of God, and the communion of Wisdom, be with you all." The same incongruity, or rather absurdity, would follow from substituting any other word expression, not of a person, but an attribute, or influence, or operation for the name of Holy Ghost, or Holy Spirit, in all the places where it occurs. We never can receive the sacred Scriptures as a certain rule of faith, intended to guide all classes of people, without admitting that the Holy Spirit is spoken of as a person. It is true, there are passages in which, if there were no others, we might be led to suppose that the Spirit was a gift, or divine influence shed on the minds of men; but all these texts can be much more easily explained, so as to harmonize with those which ascribe personal acts to the Holy Spirit, than those be reconciled to the hypothesis that the Spirit is an attribute or an influence. When we read of the Spirit dwelling in us, being given without measure, being quenched, etc., it is easy to understand that the operations and influences of this divine agent are intended.

We conclude then, that, according to a fair interpretation of the Holy Scriptures, there are three persons, each being made known by a distinct name, and to each operations and offices ascribed which are peculiar; and yet, in all works, there is a perfect concurrence of three distinct agents. As we have clear evidence that there is one God, and none beside, and as to each of the three, divine attributes are ascribed in Scripture, these three must be one God, although in what way they are one and three we do not know and do not pretend to explain. This, however, is no greater mystery than God's eternity, self-existence, and omnipresence. All we need to know is what God hath declared in His Word. Hath Christ said, "I and my Father are one" [John 10:30], and shall we not believe it, although we cannot understand nor explain how they are one? Christ says, "He that hath seen me, hath seen the Father" [John 14:9], Here are two, the Father and the Son, and yet they are so identified that he that hath seen the one hath seen the other also. Here is a fact plainly stated; this we are bound to believe; but how this can be, or what is the nature of this union, we are not required to understand, or to believe anything respecting its nature.

If the Father and the Son are one God, the Holy Spirit, to whom divine attributes and works are also ascribed, must be one with the Father and the Son. Indeed, Unitarians admit this now. They agree that the Holy Spirit is God Himself. His personality, however, they deny. But we have proved that the Holy Spirit is a person, because He is constantly spoken of as performing the acts which none but a person can perform. Let it be admitted, that the word *person*, in application to the Spirit, must not be taken in the same precise, definite sense, as when applied to men and angels, yet the Spirit searches; the Spirit understands; the Spirit speaks; the Spirit calls and appoints to the ministry; the Spirit reproves, teaches, guides, comforts, intercedes, inspires, sanctifies, and sheds abroad the love of God. The Spirit witnesses with our spirits, the Spirit quickens, the Spirit may be grieved—may be sinned against, distinctly from sins against the Son.

What an adorable being is the Triune God! How gloriously mysterious in His being, attributes, operations, and personal acts! How little are we capable of knowing of this infinite Being! None by searching can find out the Almighty to perfection [Job 11:7]. Where the feelings of the heart are right, the incomprehensible nature of the divine existence causes no obstruction to genuine devotion. Indeed, the soul of man is so constituted as to require an incomprehensible Being as the object of worship. Profound adoration is the very feeling which corresponds with this attribute. Were it not so, the angels in heaven would be perplexed and unhappy; for the more is known of God, the more mysteries are perceived in the divine character. "Clouds and darkness are round about him, righteousness and judgment are the habitation of his throne" [Ps. 97:2]. He is also represented as "dwelling in the light which no man can approach unto" [1 Tim. 6:16], and to which no mortal can approach. How condescending is God to furnish us with an object of worship in our own nature, where the attributes of deity shine forth in the face of a man like ourselves. This is truly the grand mystery of godliness: "God manifest in the flesh" [1 Tim. 3:16], "For in him dwelleth all the fulness of the Godhead bodily" [Col. 2:9], so that He is both God and man in the same person.

Perhaps this mode of exhibiting the divine attributes in humanity may be of unspeakable importance to all intelligent creatures in heaven. It may have given them an opportunity of knowing much more of God than they ever knew before, or could know in any other way. The doctrine of redemption is not only useful to the redeemed, but to all the hierarchy of heaven. No creature can know anything of the nature of God but what He is pleased to reveal; and the method by which He makes Himself known is by His works and dispensations. No creature can penetrate the divine essence, and search the deep things of God. That the Son knows the Father, as He is known by Him, furnishes a conclusive argument of His divinity. And that the Spirit searches the deep things of God, is also a sure argument of His divinity.

CHAPTER 10

Creation

The first information which the Bible gives us is of the creation of all things out of nothing in the space of six days. No other book gives any satisfactory account of the creation of the world or of the origin of the human race. The Bible does not profess to inform us when the substance of the heavens and the earth was created, but it assures us that it had a beginning, and that God was its creator. When the time arrived for the creation of man upon the earth, the confused and shapeless mass which was covered with darkness, under the forming and creative agency of the Almighty, began to assume a new appearance. The effects produced were not wrought instantly, but day after day, for six consecutive days. On the first day, light was created, for, "God said Let there be light: and there was light" [Gen. 1:3]. On the second day, God formed the firmament, or atmosphere, which separated the water in the seas from that held suspended in the clouds, or invisibly in the air. On the third day, the waters were collected into the basin prepared for them, and were separated from the earth, or dry land, which now became visible; also on this day, the earth was planted with every kind of herb yielding seed, and trees yielding fruit after their kinds respectively, with the power of propagating their species. On the fourth day, the luminaries of heaven were formed, or then began to shine upon the earth: the sun to rule the day, the moon, and the stars to rule the night. If it be asked how light could exist and form the day before the creation of the sun, it must be confessed that our knowledge of the elements of matter is very indistinct and imperfect. The question proceeds on the supposition that light is a substance which comes out of the sun by emanation; but it is much more reasonable to believe that light is nothing more than a certain condition of a widely diffused fluid, which when excited, produces in us the sense of sight; just as another fluid, when agitated, by its undulations produces in us the sense of hearing. On this subject we assert nothing; but if the theory mentioned will remove the difficulty, it is a proper answer to the question. But even if the sun were a body of light, the substance of light might have been created before it was conglomerated into one great body; or, the sun might not have been visible until the fourth day. On the fifth day, the water and air were replenished with living inhabitants, with constitutions, instincts, and senses exactly suited to the element in which they were placed. On the sixth day, the earth was stocked with beasts and reptiles of every species.

Finally, a council was called in heaven, when the crowning work of creation was about to be produced; that is, the adorable Trinity deliberated, speaking after the manner of men: "And God said, Let us make man in our image, after our likeness: and let them have dominion over the fish of the sea, and over the fowl of the air, and over the cattle, and over all the earth, and over every creeping thing that creepeth upon the earth" [Gen. 1:26].

As God is a spirit, and has no bodily parts, what is here said of His "image and likeness" must relate to His spiritual and moral nature. As man was created an immortal, intelligent spirit, in this respect, he bears a resemblance to his Creator; but we have stronger evidence for referring these words to the moral image of God. For the apostle Paul, when speaking of the renewal of man in the image of God, makes it to consist in "righteousness and true holiness" (Eph. 4:24). And, in another place, he makes this image to consist in knowledge: "And have put on the new man which is renewed in knowledge, after the image of him that created him" [Col. 3:10], in which last words there is a plain reference to the history of man's creation in Genesis.

But as it was not judged to be good that man should be alone, his Creator, in great kindness, formed for him a suitable companion, a woman taken from his own side, a help meet for him, and the mother of all living. To the man was given the name Adam, meaning "red," and to the woman the name Eve, which signifies "living."

God pronounced all that He had created "good" and "very good" [Gen. 1:31]. Nothing imperfect ever came from the hands of God. All creatures were not made equal, and in respect to constitution some are more perfect than others; but everything is perfect in its kind. In creation, as far as it is subjected to our view, there is a beautiful gradation of creatures from the most exalted angel down to the minutest atom; and among animated creatures there is a scale of perfection, according to which one living creature rises above another by almost insensible degrees. And among the creatures there is observable a mutual dependence of one upon another, and in the whole there is an astonishing harmony; or if there should be the appearance of disorder and confusion in some things, it must be attributed to our ignorance. For as far as we can understand the works of God, everything seems to be in its proper place, and governed by laws adapted to its nature.

CHAPTER 11

Good Angels

Although reason cannot assure us that there are, in the universe, creatures of an order superior to man, yet all analogy is favorable to such a doctrine. As we find that below the human race, there is a gradation of animated beings, down to the lowest forms of organized life, it would be strange indeed if the infinite space above man should be entirely unoccupied. And as the deity is a pure spirit, without bodily parts, it would seem reasonable to think that He has made some species of creatures of a purely spiritual essence. These remarks are made because Rationalists are generally disposed to deny the real existence of angels; whereas, professing to be guided by reason, they ought readily to receive this doctrine, which is so clearly revealed in the Bible. It may properly be mentioned here that Jews, Mohammedans, and Pagans, all concur in believing in a species of creatures of nobler capacities than belong to the human race. This almost universal agreement is probably derived from ancient tradition, but if from the suggestions of reason, it is still favorable to the doctrine of Scripture on this subject.

The word translated *angel* properly means, *a messenger*. It is, therefore, frequently applied to human beings, in which cases it is literally translated *messenger*. And not only so, but we have abundant proof that the word is also used to designate the Son of God, the angel that appeared to Abraham, and is expressly called Jehovah; also, the same that spoke to Moses from the burning bush, and said, "I am the God of Abraham, Isaac, and Jacob" [Exod. 3:6], who is also called an angel. This is the angel who led the Israelites through the wilderness by a fiery pillar and a protecting cloud, and often appeared to them in glory, at the tabernacle. This was the angel in whom was "the name of Jehovah," and who is called by Malachi, "the messenger," or "angel of the covenant" [Mal. 3:1].

Many theologians have also maintained that Michael the Archangel was not a created being, but the Son of God; for this opinion, however, the reasons are not conclusive. There is no propriety in speaking of archangels, for only one is ever mentioned in the Holy Scriptures.

There can be no doubt that angels are created beings, although we are not informed when they were brought into existence. It is probable, however, that the whole universe, with all the various species of beings, was produced at once, since the whole appears to form one grand system. But we must not pretend to be wise above what is written.

Angels are moral agents and accountable beings, or they could not be holy, and could not have sinned, as many of them have done. When created, they were doubtless placed in a state of probation as man was. Indeed, every rational creature, made under a moral law, is naturally in a state of probation; that is, obedience is required of him, a reward promised, and a penalty threatened in case of disobedience. All creatures are mutable; therefore, all creatures, however exalted, are capable of sinning when left to themselves. Unless God, in infinite kindness and condescension, limited the period of probation, it would last forever; as forever, the creature left to himself would be liable to sin. But, it has pleased the goodness of God to limit the probation of His moral subjects to a certain period, probably short, after which, those who stand the trial and retain their integrity, are confirmed in a state of immutable holiness and happiness. Those angels who kept their first estate, and resisted the temptation by which many of their companions were seduced from their allegiance, are not only called "holy angels" [Matt. 25:31; Mark 8:38; Luke 9:26; Rev. 14:10], but "elect angels" [1 Tim. 5:21]. What proportion of the number fell is not revealed, though the Romanists pretend to determine this and many other points, for which they have no authority from Scripture. The number of good angels, we know, is very great. Christ said that He could pray to His Father, and He would send to His aid more than twelve legions of angels, which would be more than seventy thousand. And at the birth of our Savior, there were present with the shepherds, a great multitude of the heavenly host. In the book of Daniel and of the Revelation, we read of "thousands of thousands and ten thousand times ten thousand" [Rev. 5:11]. In Hebrews 12:22, the apostle speaks of "an innumerable company of angels."

Angels are possessed of wisdom and intelligence superior to that of man, and continually contemplate the divine glory as manifested in the work of creation, and especially, in the work of redemption. "Which things," says Peter, "the angels desire to look into" [1 Pet. 1:12]. In the Revelation of John, they are represented as

encircling the throne of the Almighty, and ascribing
unto Him that sitteth on the throne and to the Lamb
"power, and riches, and wisdom, and strength, and
honour, and glory, and blessing" [Rev. 5:12].

That the angels are guardians of the children of
God, is clearly taught in the Holy Scriptures. "The angel of the Lord encampeth around them that fear him
and delivereth them (Ps. 34:7). "For he shall give his
angels charge over thee, to keep thee in all thy ways.
They shall bear thee up in their hands, lest thou dash
thy foot against a stone" (Ps. 91:11-12). And it seems
to be intimated by our Savior that particular angels
have the charge of individuals; for when speaking of
children that believe, He says, "Take heed that ye de-
spise not one of these little ones, for I say unto you,
That in heaven their angels do always behold the face
of my Father which is in heaven" (Matt. 18:10). But
whether every saint has an angel to attend him alone,
although not revealed, is improbable; for aught we
know, one guardian angel may be sufficient for many
individuals. Neither is it necessary to suppose that
guardian angels are always present with their wards;
it is sufficient that they frequently visit them.

It would seem clear from Scripture that all the holy
angels are occupied in this service; for in the epistle to
the Hebrews, we read, "Are they not all ministering
spirits, sent forth to minister for them who shall be
heirs of salvation?" (Heb. 1:14). The Romanists, indeed,
confine this ministry to the very lowest of the nine
orders of their celestial hierarchy; but for their doctrine, they have no solid foundation, and it is refuted
by the declaration of our Lord, already quoted, that the
guardian angels of the little ones who believe do always

behold the face of God in heaven. These must, there-fore, be of the highest order; and the word *angels*, in the New Testament, is a general term, comprehending all orders.

This leads us at once to the inquiry whether there are different ranks and orders of good angels. While we reject the hierarchy of the Romish priests, which has no foundation in Scripture, we cannot but admit that according to the testimony of Paul there are several ranks, or orders of angels; but how they differ from one another, we cannot tell. All we know is that the names by which they are designated and distinguished import high station, and great power and dignity. They are called, "thrones, dominions, principalities, and powers," but exalted as they are, the Son of God is declared to be their Creator.

As the word "angel" signifies a messenger, some are of the opinion that the "spirits of just men made per-fect" [Heb. 12:23] may be of the number employed in missions to the earth, especially as guardians. But no-thing of this kind can be learned from the sacred Scriptures.

CHAPTER 12

Bad Angels

There is an evil being, often mentioned in Scripture, both in the Old and New Testaments called Satan, the devil, Beelzebub, and other significant names. But he is always spoken of as one, the original Greek for devil (Διαβολος) never being found in the plural to signify devils, though the plural is used in the New Testament for slanderers. It is true, the word devils in the plural is often read in our version; but the original thus translated is an entirely different word, and would more properly be rendered *demons*. From this some have been disposed to maintain that these demons were of an entirely different nature from the person called Diabolus and Satan; and some have conjectured that they were the departed spirits of wicked men. But there is little foundation in the Scriptures for these conjectures. Satan is no doubt greatly superior to all the other evil spirits; but whether of a different species we cannot tell. One individual of the same species may be endowed with powers far above the rest. An opinion which has more probability is that Satan, in a state of innocence, was an archangel, or prince over a large number of the celestial host; and that by his influence, those subject to his authority were seduced from their allegiance, and fell with him in the same transgression. For he is still called "the prince of the devils" [Matt.

9:34; Matt. 12:24; Mark 3:22], "the god of this world" [2 Cor. 4:4], "the prince of the power of the air, the spirit that now worketh in the children of disobedience" [Eph. 2:2], and "the adversary that walketh about, seeking whom he may devour" [1 Pet. 5:8].

Coming nearer to the point, we read of hell being originally prepared for "the devil and his angels" [Matt. 25:41]. As we know that evil spirits are very numerous, we may infer that they are all in subjection to this prince of darkness, whether willingly or unwillingly, it would be vain to inquire. And this will account for that which to many has appeared difficult to be understood, how Satan can tempt so many persons all over the world at once; it would seem, at first view, that he is omnipresent. But if he has at his command thousands of emissaries, or even if this host of evil spirits act independently of him, the difficulty will be removed. It ought, however, to be remembered that a spirit can pass from place to place more rapidly than the light; and Satan may be carrying on his temptations in America this moment, and the next he may be in Europe, and then in Africa or Asia, and back again, in the twinkling of an eye.

The Scriptures make it certain that our first parents were seduced by the devil in the form of the serpent; and that the curse denounced on the serpent related chiefly to him. In the book of Revelation, he is called "that old serpent, called the Devil" [Rev. 12:9; Rev. 20:2], and our Lord declared that "he was a murderer from the beginning" [John 8:44], and "a liar and the father of it," which can have no other reference than to the bringing of death on our first parents, and their posterity, and to the lie—the first ever told in this world—by which he deceived the woman, when he said, "Ye shall not surely die" [Gen. 3:4]. And for these reasons he is called "a murderer" and "the father of lies."

How great his malice is against the people of God and what injuries he would inflict upon them, if permitted, may be learned from the book of Job.

At the advent of our Savior, he seems to have been let loose in an unusual manner; for "the Son of God was manifested, that he might destroy the works of the devil" [1 John 3:8], and therefore the powers of darkness were permitted to exert their malice and cunning in a degree greater than at any other period. As Christ came to accomplish a salvation which the first Adam had failed to secure, there was a propriety in His being exposed to the temptations of the same adversary who had overcome our first representative. Accordingly, Satan made an insidious attack on our Lord, as soon as He came up from the waters of baptism, and He was led into the wilderness by the Spirit for this very purpose. But in this assault, Satan was completely repulsed; and when our Substitute died on the cross, which Satan had brought about by entering into Judas, the serpent's head was completely bruised by the Seed of the woman, while he could do no more than bruise the heel of the God-man Mediator. In the view of this victory, Christ said, on a certain occasion, "I beheld Satan as lightning fall from heaven" [Luke 10:18]. And again, "The prince of this world is judged" [John 16:11].

While Christ was on earth, many persons were possessed of demons, who, entering into them, agitated and convulsed their bodies in a very hideous manner; and so governed the bodies of the miserable sufferers that they became mere instruments of the evil spirits, who made use of their tongues to utter what the demons wished. The power of our Savior was manifested, frequently and triumphantly, in ejecting the unclean spirits from the bodies in which they had taken up their abode. Sometimes, many would take possession of one person. In one case, a certain demoniac, upon being asked his name, answered, *"Legion*: for we are many"* [Mark 5:9]. And in another case, seven devils were cast out of one woman, who became eminent for her tender love to her Savior. And our Lord mentions a case where a demon, for a time, left the person possessed, and wandering about in dry places, and finding no rest, said, "I will return into my house from whence I came out; and when he is come, he findeth it empty, swept, and garnished. Then goeth he, and taketh with himself seven other spirits more wicked than himself, and they enter in and dwell there: and the last state of that man is worse than the first" [Matt 12:44-45; Luke 11:24-26].

We are not to suppose that the mere demoniacal possession of a person was a crime, or that what was said or done by a demoniac, would be charged on the man or woman possessed; but these possessions were probably the punishment of sins which they had committed; or, as in the case of the blind man, "that the works of God should be made manifest in them" [John 9:3]. Because the effects produced on the human body by these possessions greatly resemble certain diseases, such as insanity and epilepsy, to which the human frame is subject, some learned men have maintained that what are called demoniacal possessions in the New Testament were nothing but incurable diseases,

and allege that the miracle is as real upon this hypothesis, as on the other. This is true; but the objection
to this opinion is that it undermines the truth of the
gospel history. If nothing more was said than that
certain demoniacs were healed, this hypothesis might
be admitted. For we read that among others who were
healed by our Savior, were *lunatics*, and yet, no edu-
cated man now believes that madness is produced by
the moon. But in regard to demoniacal possessions, the
evangelists relate conversations which passed between
them and our Lord; and, in one instance, where there
were many in one man, they entreated that they might
not be sent out of the country, but should be permitted
to enter into a numerous herd of swine, which were on
the mountain, near the lake. Permission being given,
the herd of swine ran violently down a precipice into
the sea, and were drowned.

If all this is to be taken as a mere accommodation
to Jewish prejudices, then we can have no certainty of
any of the facts related by the evangelists. And, indeed,
the censure would fall back on our Savior himself, who
continually speaks of demoniacs as persons really possessed by unclean spirits. As a further proof of the
reality of such possessions, it may be remarked, that
the demons acknowledged Christ to be the Son of God;
and that in a country where the people knew him not,
and begged him to depart from their coasts. It is expressly said, that upon the approach of Jesus, the demon cried out, "What have I to do with thee, Jesus,
thou Son of the most high God? I adjure thee by God,
that thou torment me not" [Mark 5:7; Luke 8:28]. And
he asked him, "What is thy name?" and he answered,
saying, "My name is Legion: for we are many. And he

besought him much that he would not send them away out of the country. Now there was there nigh unto the mountains a great herd of swine feeding. And all the devils besought him, saying, Send us into the swine, that we may enter into them. And forthwith Jesus gave them leave, and the unclean spirits went out, and entered into the swine: and the herd ran violently down a steep place into the sea" [Mark 5:9-13].

Now, if any one, upon a careful perusal of this narrative, can persuade himself that these were no real spirits, but that it was simply a case of insanity, and that demons are introduced in accommodation to the common prejudices of the Jews, he will have adopted a principle of interpretation which will go far towards subverting the whole gospel history. For, why may it not be as reasonably supposed that when Christ speaks of the resurrection of the body, or of a future judgment, He is merely uttering opinions common among the Pharisees, the predominant sect of the Jews? In answer to the allegation that the symptoms were precisely the same, as of diseases which are still often encountered, it may be replied that the demons might be permitted to produce these very diseases, as we know that these malignant spirits are capable of producing diseases of any kind, if permitted without restraint to operate with the power which naturally belongs to them, as we see in the case of Job and of the woman healed by our Savior on the Sabbath day, "whom," said He, "Satan hath bound, lo, these eighteen years" [Luke 13:16]. In some of these diseases, as they now occur, we know too little about their real causes to make it the ground for argument. Physicians are very little acquainted with the causes of diseases of every species. All they can ascertain by the most accurate examination is the disease itself, or the derangement of some part of the human system. But in many cases, they can acquire no knowledge of the cause of that disorder; and for all that we know, evil spirits may now, sometimes, have a power over the bodies of men, by permission. We do not assert this as a fact, but only that the thing is not impossible, nor altogether improbable.

But our principal concern with the existence of evil spirits does not relate to their power to injure the body, but their cunning and malice in tempting men to sin. As Satan tempted our Lord, so he tempted the disciples. He took complete possession of Judas, by his consent, and induced him to commit the most enormous crime on record. He also tempted Peter, and for a season overcame him. Had he not been preserved from utter apostasy by the intercession of his Lord, we have reason to think that his case would have been as desperate as that of Judas. Christ says, "Simon, Simon, behold, Satan hath desired to have you, that he may sift you as wheat, but I have prayed for thee, that thy faith fail not" [Luke 22:31-32]. And when Ananias and Sapphira were guilty of an enormous crime, in lying to the Holy Ghost, Peter, in his address, said, "Why hath Satan filled thine heart to lie to the Holy Ghost?" [Acts 5:3].

That true believers have to endure a severe conflict with these powers of darkness is exceedingly evident from what Paul says in his Epistle to the Ephesians. "Put on the whole armour of God, that ye may be able to stand against the wiles of the devil. For we wrestle not against flesh and blood, but against principalities, against powers, against the rulers of the darkness of this world, against spiritual wickedness in high places"

[Eph. 6:11-12]. He exhorts, to take "the shield of faith, wherewith ye shall be able to quench all the fiery darts of the wicked" [Eph. 6:16]. It is hence manifest that Christians are surrounded by a host of spiritual enemies, of whom the devil is the leader; and it would seem that there are the same orders among the fallen as among the blessed angels. They are described as "principalities, powers, and rulers, and as spiritual wickedness in high places." And in 2 Corinthians 2:11, Paul cautions those to whom he wrote, "Lest Satan should get an advantage of us; for we are not ignorant of his devices."

And Peter recognizes the existence and malice of the same invisible enemy, in his exhortation to Christians: "Be sober, be vigilant; because your adversary the devil, as a roaring lion, walketh about, seeking whom he may devour" [1 Pet. 5:8]. And Paul exhorts the Ephesians, "Neither give place to the devil" [Eph. 4:27], that is, do not yield to him; resist him. The same exhortation, in substance, is given by James. "Resist the devil, and he will flee from you" [James 4:7]. This doctrine of spiritual enemies watching our path and seeking our destruction is, at first view, very appalling; until we recollect, that the Captain of our salvation is able to bruise Satan under our feet; yea, He has already conquered him, and has him completely under His control, and has promised to His people that they shall not be "tempted above that ye are able," and that "with the temptation" He will "make a way to escape" [1 Cor. 10:13].

But if the real Christian is thus exposed to the temptations of the evil one, what must be the condition of impenitent men? The Scriptures are also very explicit and full on this point. They are said to be "taken captive by him at his will" [2 Tim. 2:26]. Those who are "dead in trespasses and sins" [Eph. 2:1], are described as walking "according to the course of this world, according to the prince of the power of the air, the spirit that now worketh in the children of disobedience" [Eph. 2:2]. When the gospel is preached, Satan taketh away the word that was sown in the hearts of the hearers. He is also said to have "blinded the minds of them which believe not, lest the light of the glorious gospel of Christ, who is the image of God, should shine unto them" [2 Cor. 4:4]. And when men are converted, they are translated from the power of darkness into the kingdom of God's dear Son. "He that committeth sin is of the devil, for the devil sinneth from the beginning" [1 John 3:8]. "Ye are of your father the devil, and the lusts of your father ye will do" [John 8:44]. "When a strong man armed keepeth his palace, his goods are in peace" [Luke 11:21]. Wretched, indeed, is the condition of those who are under the power of such a malignant spirit. They are willing slaves to the most cruel of masters.

CHAPTER 13

Providence of God

The providence of God is "his most holy, wise, and powerful preserving and governing all his creatures and all their actions" [SC 11].

All creatures are necessarily dependent on the Creator for their continued existence. If He should withdraw His supporting hand, they would cease to be. If we admit that God in wisdom made the world, He had some end in view in the works which by His power He produced. It is most certain, therefore, that He will so direct and govern His creatures that the end designed shall be accomplished. Being perfect in wisdom and power, He is able to order all events and the actions of all creatures in such a manner as to attain the end which He purposed to Himself in the beginning. To suppose that His purpose failed of its accomplishment, or that the actual state of things in the universe is different from the original plan of the Creator, would be attended with so many absurd consequences that the idea should not for a moment be admitted. Such an opinion would detract essentially from the wisdom or power of the Creator, and would destroy all confidence in Him as the Governor of the world; for if disconcerted and disappointed in the execution of His plan, in one instance, there can be no security that the same will not happen again and again, until everything would fall into disorder, so that the end proposed to Himself by the Creator would be forever frustrated.

The only reason that has induced any to entertain the opinion that the plan of the Almighty has been disconcerted is the introduction of sin into the world by the actions of free agents. It has been assumed as a principle that God is not only not the author of sin, which is true, but that, consistently with His holiness, He could not form a purpose that it should be permitted to exist. Though the motive which has led many to maintain that sin has come into the world in opposition to the purpose of God is good, yet the opinion is utterly untenable, being inconsistent with the perfections of Jehovah. It would make it necessary to believe not only that He did not design that evil should exist, but that He did not foresee the event. For had He foreseen it He could have prevented it, if in no other way than by omitting to bring into existence a creature capable of frustrating His plan; or by producing a creature who He foreknew would not transgress.

We must believe, therefore, that the purposes of God cannot fail of their accomplishment, and hence that He not only foresaw, but determined to suffer His creatures, in the exercise of their freedom, to commit sin. Yet this permission does not imply that He was the author of sin, or that He can look upon it with the least favor or approbation; for sin is ever that abominable thing which God hates. But He permitted free agents to commit sin; that is, He did not interpose to hinder them from acting as they pleased, because He knew that He could make the existence of sin and misery, the occasion of more illustriously displaying His attributes, particularly His justice and His mercy, than could have been done in other circumstances. The reason then, why sin was permitted to exist was that God might have an opportunity of manifesting His own glory to all intelligent creatures more conspicuously, which is the great end of all His works and dispensations.

The providence of God in regard to sin consists, first, in His purpose to permit free agents, in the exercise of their freedom, to commit sin; secondly, in so directing and governing sinful creatures, that their actions may be made subservient to His own wise purposes; and when they would not have this tendency they are restrained, according to that declaration in Psalm 76:10, "Surely the wrath of man shall praise thee: the remainder of wrath shalt thou restrain." The Holy Scriptures constantly represent the providence of God as concerned in the evil actions of men, not as causing or approving them, but as permitting, governing, and directing them, so that they may promote His own glory. Thus, the envy of Joseph's brethren, which led them to sell him as a slave, was overruled to be the occasion of preserving the whole family from death. The crucifixion of our Lord was by the hands of wicked men, in the free indulgence of their own malice, but it was nevertheless "by the determinate counsel and foreknowledge of God" [Acts 2:23]. And the same is true of all sinful actions; they are hateful to God, considered in their own nature, and yet His providence is concerned in their permission and direction, so as to promote a good end. The providence of God, therefore, in its relation to the sins of men, is most holy and wise, and does not interfere in the least with man's free agency. He "worketh all things after the counsel of his own will" [Eph. 1:11] and his "counsel shall stand" [Isa. 46:10]. "Shall there be evil in a city, and the Lord hath not done it?" (Amos 3:6).

The providence of God extends to all events, great and small. Both reason and revelation teach this doctrine. For if God governs the world at all, His providence must extend to small things as well as to great because of the concatenation of events, according to which the great often depend for their existence on the small. And if reason were silent, the Scriptures speak out clearly on this point. "The lot is cast into the lap, but the whole disposal thereof is of the Lord" [Prov. 16:33]. "Are not two sparrows sold for a farthing? and one of them shall not fall on the ground without your Father" [Matt. 10:29]. "But the very hairs of your head are all numbered" [Matt. 10:30; Luke 12:7].

As it is a most reasonable truth, so the doctrine of a particular superintending providence, is a most comfortable truth. If anything could occur without being included in the plan of the divine government, we never could feel that we are safe. The sure ground of our trust in God is that He "worketh all things according to the counsel of his own will" [Eph. 1:11]. When the dark and cloudy day of adversity comes, and billow after billow rolls over us, and threatens to overwhelm us, our consolation is that our God rides on the whirlwind and directs the storm. We may often think with Jacob "that all these things are against us" [Gen. 42:26], but when we can view every event, however afflictive, as the appointment of our heavenly Father, we can say with Eli, "It is the Lord; let him do what seemeth him good" [1 Sam. 3:18]. It is a delightful thought to the true Christian that all events are under the government of divine providence. The book of providence, the leaves of which are successively unfolded day after day, should be carefully studied, and its indications faithfully used in directing us in the path of duty.

CHAPTER 14

Man's Primeval State

As man was created a free, moral agent, it is not only true that he was capable of being governed by a moral law, but such a law resulted necessarily from his relation to his Creator. It was his duty as it was his delight, to exercise love and every holy affection toward that Being who possesses every perfection. Although man was perfect in holiness, being created in the image of God, yet he was mutable, as being a creature; for immutability properly belongs to God only. All accountable creatures are, therefore, from their very condition, in a state of probation; that is, they are made subject to a law which they are required to obey, but which, in the exercise of their freedom, they may disobey. It cannot be doubted that man was endowed with full power to comply with all the divine requisitions. The law demanded nothing but the faithful exercise of those powers and affections which belong to human nature. The sum of all obedience was to love the Lord his God with all his heart. This was not only easy to an uncorrupted nature, but his highest happiness was connected with it. Man's probation would have continued without limit, unless God, in great condescension and kindness, had been pleased to enter into covenant with him.

The word "covenant" is to be understood in a much

more general and comprehensive sense than the common import of the English term covenant. It is a solemn transaction in which God appoints and establishes certain conditions on which man might become partaker of eternal life in heaven, secure from all danger of forfeiting his interest in the favor of God. As it pleased God that the human kind should come into the world in connection with the first man, and should proceed from him as his children, it seemed good to infinite wisdom to make him the federal head and representative of all his posterity; so that upon his rendering perfect obedience to the commandments of God, for a certain limited period, eternal life would be secured to himself and to all his natural descendants. On the other hand, if he transgressed the law given to him, his sin should be considered as the sin of the whole race; or, in other words, should be so imputed to them, as that they should be brought into existence in the same moral condition into which he should fall, and be subject to the same penalties. In order that there might be a clear and decisive test of the obedience or disobedience of man, under this covenant of works, a particular tree was selected, called on account of its use, "the tree of knowledge of good and evil" [Gen. 2:9, 17]. Although the fruit of this tree was good for food, and pleasant to the eyes, yet our first parents were forbidden to eat of it, or even to touch it; and thus it became a precise test of obedience or disobedience.

There was also another sacramental tree, called "the tree of life" [Gen. 2:9], the fruit of which was to be used to prevent all disease or tendency to death; or, more probably, to be a sign and seal of eternal life to our first parents, when their period of probation should be ended, provided they continued in obedience.

Man, when created out of the dust of the earth, was inspired with a rational and immortal soul, and placed in a pleasant garden, planted with every kind of trees bearing nutritious fruits; the temperature of which was so mild that no covering for the human body was needed. As he was without experience, all knowledge necessary for the preservation of life and the performance of duty was given to him, and among these gifts was that of speech, without which there could have been no easy interchange of sentiments, nor any considerable progress in knowledge. Man was also made lord of the creation; for God said to His newly formed creature, "Have dominion over the fish of the sea, and over the fowl of the air, and over every living thing that moveth upon the earth" [Gen. 1:28]. In this respect, also, man was the image of his Creator. It was, therefore, left to Adam to give names to every beast of the field and fowl of the air; and for this purpose they were made to pass before him, "and whatsoever Adam called every living creature, that was the name thereof" [Gen 2:19].

It would seem from the tenor of the sacred history, that God conversed freely with His creature, man, while he remained in Paradise, either by the ministry of holy angels or, more probably, by His Son, assuming by anticipation the appearance of man. But on points where the sacred Scriptures do not speak decisively, it is our wisdom to be silent.

Here we may contemplate the interesting condition of our first parents. They were holy and happy, and had nothing to fear but sin; yet, considering the natural weakness of creatures, their situation was most critical, and the everlasting interests of unnumbered millions were suspended on the fallible will of our first parents. And soon, alas, all was lost!

Upon a survey of the condition in which man was placed, when created, there are two reflections which force themselves on our minds.

1. The goodness of God to the first man and to the race. Man was indeed fearfully and wonderfully made, as to the structure and constitution of his body, and, also, as to the intellectual endowments of his mind, being enriched with the noble faculties of reason, memory, and imagination. But, above all, the goodness of the Creator is manifest in stamping upon the soul of man His own moral image, and in communicating to him all that knowledge which was requisite for the performance of duty and the enjoyment of happiness. This goodness was also conspicuous in the external provision made for the supply of all his wants, and the gratification of all his innocent desires.

2. Comparing the condition of Adam in innocence with that of man now, we may form some idea of the greatness of our loss. A withering curse has fallen upon the ground itself; man has lost his perfection of life and health, and has forfeited his immortality. But the heaviest part of the curse has lighted on his moral powers. The image of God, which was his beauty and dignity, has been effaced. Corruption and disorder have ensued; and, in the place of happiness, misery, in its multiple kinds, has seized upon him. Alas, the crown has fallen from his head, and the most fine gold has become dim!

CHAPTER 15

Law of God

An obligation to perfect obedience arises from the relation which a rational creature sustains to his Creator. The right of the Author of our being to what He has made out of nothing, is the most complete right of which we can form a conception. And, as God is infinitely excellent and glorious in His own nature, it is reasonable that He should require the supreme love of the rational creature. If we had anything better than our love and gratitude to give in return for what we have received from our Creator and Preserver, we should be under obligation to render the best which we possibly could; but since pure love is the best offering of which we are capable, God requires that. But when perfect obedience is rendered, we do not repay our debt; this never can be done. When we have done all, we have only performed our duty, and as it relates to God, are "unprofitable servants" [Luke 17:10]. When man was created, he was endowed with the necessary knowledge of God and his disposition was conformable to His law, which was written on his heart. But when man sinned, the image of God, as far as it consisted in moral likeness, was lost; but some knowledge of duty, and feeling of moral obligation remained. This, however, through ignorance and negligence, was soon so obscured that except in regard to a few great enorm-

ities, men have generally lost sight of the law of God
as a rule of duty, reaching not only to the outward actions, but to the thoughts and affections of the heart.
It became very necessary, therefore, that there should
be a new revelation of the moral law, and such a specification of particular duties, as was suited to the people
of Israel, to whom the revelation was made. This revelation was communicated by God Himself from mount
Horeb, in the midst of thunderings and lightnings and
darkness and tempest, in a voice of tremendous
majesty. The Decalogue, which contained the specifications of this moral law, was written by the finger of God
on two tables of stone, after having been uttered in a
voice of thunder from the midst of the fiery mountain.

The sum and substance of the moral law, as it relates to the inner man, is comprehended in two commandments which are recognized by our Savior as still
in force and as containing summarily all moral duty.
The first of these is, "Hear, O Israel; The Lord our God
is one Lord: and thou shalt love the Lord thy God with
all thy heart, and with all thy soul, and with all thy
mind and with all thy strength: this is the first commandment. And the second is like, namely this, Thou
shalt love thy neighbour as thyself" (Mark 12:29-31).
"On these two commandments hang all the law and
the prophets" [Matt. 22:40].

As to the dispositions and affections of heart required by this law, they are the same to all persons and
under all dispensations; but as to the external acts
required, they vary according to the relations in which
men are placed. While, therefore, the principles of
moral obedience are simple, the acts which may be incumbent on moral agents may be infinitely diversified.

All, however, in every situation, are bound externally to reverence and worship God, and to exercise justice and mercy in their intercourse with their fellow men. And there are also moral duties which have respect to ourselves. It is the duty of all, by lawful means, to seek their own welfare—the improvement of their minds, and the health and purity of their bodies; and to avoid everything which has any tendency to injure themselves. The exhortation, "Do thyself no harm" [Acts 16:28], is of general application, and is a moral duty of great importance.

It has been common to divide moral duties into three classes: those we owe to God, to our neighbor, and to ourselves. From what has been said, it is evident that there is some foundation, in the nature of the case, for this threefold distinction. But it seems scarcely correct to speak of owing duties to our fellow creatures or to ourselves, as though we had more sovereigns than one. There is, strictly speaking, but one Sovereign and one Judge to whom we owe allegiance. We are bound to love our neighbor because God enjoins it, and to promote our own welfare for the same reason. We are under one moral law, which is binding because it is made known to us to be the will of God. It is obvious that when all internal holiness is comprehended in love, this word must be taken in a generic sense to include all right affections toward God and toward our fellow creatures, such as reverence, trust, gratitude, etc.; and a like latitude should be given to it in relation to our fellow men.

The law of God is perfect. It has been justly called a transcript of the moral perfections of God. It is the highest standard of moral dignity and excellence, of which the creature is capable. It is also the measure of man's supreme happiness. We see then, not only that it is just in God to require perfect obedience to the law, and that to require less would be a derogation from His holiness; but that His goodness is equally manifest in the requisition of all the love and obedience of which the nature of man is susceptible; for it is that very state of mind in which man's purest and sublimest happiness consists. And if we should, for a moment, suppose that a less degree of love and obedience should be required, either as to intensity or constancy, where would we fix this degree? It is evident that in proportion as man falls short of perfect love, or that degree of love to his Creator, of which he is constitutionally capable, so far he sinks in moral dignity and excellence. And no man can fix any other measure of love which might not be, on the same principle, lowered more and more, until nothing was left.

But the law of God is also just, for it requires no more than what the creature, as he came from the hands of his Creator, had full power to render. In the case of all creatures in innocence, the maxim is correct that duty and ability must be commensurate. Accordingly, God does not require man to love or obey with the powers of an angel, but to love the Lord his God with all his heart, mind, and strength. But this maxim cannot with propriety be applied to the case of those who by their own fault have lost the ability of rendering perfect obedience. The law of God cannot lower its demands in proportion to the inability of man, brought on by transgression. That blindness of mind, hardness of heart, and perversity of will pro-duced by sinning, are in themselves sinful, and cannot, therefore, furnish any excuse. In fact, these things constitute the root and core of our depravity, and are the very things for which man shall chiefly be condemned. The same is true of inveterate habits of sin and of errors which are the fruit of sin. These things cannot excuse, or there would be no blame anywhere. No moral change, however, affects the essence of the soul; its faculties remain the same under all moral conditions. Sin destroys no constitutional faculty, and regeneration produces no new faculty. Man, in all stages of his existence, continues to be a free moral agent. If this were not the case, he could not be the subject of a moral government. Whatever the law requires, therefore, man has the mental faculties which are sufficient for its performance, if they were under the direction and government of right dispositions of heart. These things being rightly understood, the difficulty and perplexity often experienced in regard to man's being required to perform what he has no power to perform, will be removed.

Besides those duties which arise out of our natural relations, and which are called moral, God may prescribe other actions, commanding the creature to perform acts, or abstain from acts, which in themselves are indifferent, that is, destitute of a moral character. These acts when commanded or forbidden, are as really binding on the conscience as those dictated by reason, for, whatever is known to be the will of God is law, and obligatory. The only difference between duties of this class and others is that the obligation rests simply on the revealed will of God. Having nothing of a holy or sinful nature considered in themselves, they may be changed or abolished at the pleasure of the

Sovereign. But moral duties are, in the same relations, and under the same circumstances, immutable; they cannot be dispensed with. This lays a foundation for the distinction between moral and positive precepts. The first God must require, or cease to be holy; the last are binding when commanded, but may be changed or abolished by the Lawgiver, according to His wisdom and pleasure. It is not to be understood, however, that ceremonial, or positive precepts have nothing of a moral nature. The difference between moral and positive duties is merely in the external act; but as to the motive and end, there is no difference whatever. God's commands must be obeyed from love to Him, and with a view to His glory, of whatever kind they be.

The decalogue, or Ten Commandments, should be considered as a general specification of the duties arising out of the usual relations in which men stand; and not intended to express every particular species of duty, or every conceivable kind of sin. Such a law, thus carried out in minute detail, would be useless by its bulk, and by the multiplicity of particulars would distract, rather than direct. The method chosen is by far more consonant with wisdom, where the principles of moral duty are clearly laid down, and such a number of specifications given, as will enable the conscientious reader or hearer to form a correct judgment respecting similar cases.

The following rules have been given as useful in the explanation of the Decalogue.

1. The law is spiritual, and extends not only to the external acts of the body, but to the thoughts, desires, and purposes of the heart or mind. Paul, in Romans 7:14, testifies that the law is spiritual. "For we know

that the law is spiritual." "Nay, I had not known sin, but by the law: for I had not known lust, except the law had said, Thou shalt not covet" [Rom. 7:7]. The same thing may be conclusively argued from the character of the Lawgiver, who is holy, and whose prerogative it is to search the heart. In the common judgment of mankind, the good or evil of an act must be traced to the motive and the purpose of the agent. Civil rulers can only take cognizance of overt acts, but God judges the heart. Hence it often happens that that which is highly esteemed among men is an abomination in the sight of God; because man looks on the outward appearance, but God looks on the heart. And this is strongly confirmed and illustrated in our Savior's exposition of the true nature of the law, where He represents malice to possess the guilt of murder, and a wanton eye that of adultery.

2. In affirmative precepts, negative must be considered as included; and *vice versa*, negative in affirmative.

In many passages of Scripture, much more is meant than is explicitly expressed. But in the application of this rule caution and sound judgment are requisite, lest we make the law a nose of wax, which can be bent into any shape—a vague and indefinite thing, which every one may understand in that sense which suits him. We must inquire accurately and profoundly into the mind of the Legislator as elsewhere expressed, and pay strict attention to the context and to the occasion on which any precept was spoken.

It is plain, however, that a precept enjoining something good, cannot be obeyed without avoiding the contrary evil. It is also evident that when any particular sin is forbidden, obedience cannot be rendered, without cultivating and practicing the contrary virtue. Thus, when it is said, "Thou shalt not kill" [Exod. 20:13], it is evident that it is implied, that we should not only refrain from injuring our neighbor, but should do what we can to promote his welfare. And the command not to steal includes an obligation to advance, as far as it may be in our power, our neighbor's property and outward estate. And every one sees that the command to honor our parents includes a prohibition to dishonor or injure them.

3. In each of the commandments it is necessary to suppose that, for brevity's sake, a part is put for the whole; a specimen which may be said to represent all duties or sins of the same class. The prohibition of any sin includes all things which would tend toward it, and all inclinations leading to its commission. Thus, when it is said, "Thou shalt not commit adultery" [Exod. 20:14], all impure conduct is forbidden, as sodomy, incest, fornication, and all lascivious actions; also all unchaste thoughts, imaginations, and desires which lead to the commission of the crimes that belong to this class.

4. The cause must be considered as included in the effect, the genus in the species, and the correlative in the relative. Thus, in the prohibition of stealing, covetousness, its cause, is forbidden. In the prohibition of murder, cherished anger is included. Under the head of theft, every species of fraud and injustice is included. Under the sin of "taking the name of the Lord in vain" [Exod. 20:7] is included all profaneness and lack of due reverence for anything relating to God, such as all trifling and jesting with His Word, and all ridicule or contempt of the worship and ordinances of His house.

So also, when the duty of children to parents is

enjoined, the correlative duties of parents to their children must be considered as required. And the mention of one class of relative duties, must be considered as a specimen of all relative duties. It is right, therefore, under the fifth commandment, to comprehend the duties of magistrates and subjects, of masters and servants, of pastors and their flocks, of husbands and wives, and of every relation which lawfully exists among men.

There are two rules laid down by theologians on this subject, which though generally true, cannot be considered as universally applicable.

5. The one is that the duties of the first table, or those which have God for their object, should have preference above those of the second table, which have our fellow men for their object. But if a man be in danger of perishing, and we can save his life by omitting prayer, or the worship of God, it is obviously our duty to give preference to the duty of saving the life of a fellow creature. Many other cases might be supposed.

6. The second rule, commonly laid down, and which is not of universal application, is that moral duties take the preference over positive; mercy must be preferred to sacrifice. For this we have the authority of the prophets and our Savior Himself: "I will have mercy and not sacrifice" [Matt. 9:13].

Neither must this rule be considered as universally applicable. Indeed, we cannot in any case determine our duty by it, without regard to the nature and circumstances of the duties which may come into competition; for where there is no inconsistency in performing the duties, both kinds are obligatory, though some may be much more important than others. The Pharisees who neglected the weightier matters of the law, and were scrupulous in observing the payment of tithes, even on the herbs of the garden, are not blamed for tithing mint, anise, and cummin, but for neglecting much more important duties, as appears by the words of our Savior, "These ought ye to have done, and not to leave the other undone" [Matt. 23:23].

But when moral and positive duties interfere, the question is whether the moral must in all cases have the precedence. That mercy should be preferred to sacrifice is clearly revealed, but that in every case a divinely appointed ordinance must give way to every species of moral duty cannot properly be inferred from this text. Suppose a believer to be so situated that he has the opportunity of receiving Christian baptism, or attending the Lord's Supper, and to be under the necessity of going on a tedious voyage to sea, would it be his duty to neglect either of these holy sacraments, for the sake of performing some moral act not of the first importance, which could not be performed, unless he would omit these positive duties? For example, suppose that just when about to attend the Lord's Supper, he should be sent for, to visit a sick person at a distance, would he be bound to neglect the only opportunity he might ever have to receive either of the sacraments of the Christian church? I think not. Indeed, to Christians, as commonly situated, it would not be proper to absent themselves from the table of the Lord, in order to pull an ox or sheep out of a pit, into which it had fallen; though this is a moral duty, when not called to the performance of other duties, which are more important.

Why the ceremonies of religion are sometimes spoken of in a disparaging way was on account of the total defect of spirituality. As Isaiah says, "To what purpose is the multitude of your sacrifices unto me? saith the Lord: I am full of the burnt offerings of rams, and the fat of fed beasts, and I delight not in the blood of bullocks; or of lambs, or of he goats. When ye come to appear before me, who hath required this at your hand, to tread my courts?" [Isa. 1:11-12]. And again, "He that killeth an ox is as if he slew a man; he that sacrificeth a lamb, as if he cut off a dog's neck; he that offereth an oblation, as if he offered swine's blood; he that burneth incense, as if he blessed an idol" [Isa. 66:3]. The reason why appointed rites are thus spoken of as services condemned and spurned by the Almighty, is not because the right performance of the ceremonial law was not acceptable, but because the people utterly neglected the moral and spiritual part of worship, which is its essence, and depended entirely on the performance of external rites. Meanwhile they indulged without restraint their wicked inclinations; vainly trusting that these observances would be a compensation for all moral defects.

7. Another rule which has been given for the interpretation of the moral law is, "That affirmative precepts are always obligatory, but do not require a constant performance; whereas negative precepts are not only always obligatory, but must be constantly observed." This rule, though true, is of very little use, as the direction contained in it is obvious to the reason of every reflecting man. The duty of prayer is always obligatory, but not a duty to be performed at all times; but the negative precept, forbidding us to take the name of the Lord in vain, binds us always, and is always to be observed.

The moral law will be better understood by considering the nature of the obedience which it demands;

and this may be comprehended in the following particulars.

I. The law reaches to the whole of man; to the soul with all its faculties, and to the body with all its members.

II. A fourfold perfection is required by the law.
1. It must be cordial or from the heart.
2. Universal, both as to its object and its parts.
3. In the degree of its intensity—with all the heart, etc.
4. In its duration; it must never cease.

8. The beginning, middle, and end of obedience is love out of a pure heart and faith unfeigned. But under the term love is comprehended, as was said before, every virtuous feeling and holy purpose and emotion. When the word is thus taken, "love is the fulfilling of the law" [Rom. 13:10], the two commandments in which all others are included are love to God and love to our neighbor. As on these hang all the law and the prophets, that is, all incumbent duties, in them must be included all holy affections toward God, and all right dispositions toward our fellow creatures, according to our relation to them and our opportunity of doing them good, "for love worketh no ill to his neighbour."

CHAPTER 16

Fall of Man

How long our first parents continued in innocence we are not informed, and it would be in vain to conjecture; but the common opinion has been that the time was short.

An enemy of God already existed—a fallen spirit, who had led a multitude of his fellow angels into rebellion; they were cast out of their celestial habitations, but had liberty, for a season, to roam about the universe of God. Satan, the prince of the devils, envying the happiness of man, formed the design of seducing him from his allegiance, and bringing him into the same degraded and wretched condition with himself. He, therefore, watched his opportunity, and knowing the woman to be the "weaker vessel" [1 Pet. 3:7], he resolved to make his first assault on her. She seems to have been curiously gazing on the beautiful fruit of the forbidden tree, when the arch-fiend, making use of the body of the serpent, which was the wisest of the animal tribes and originally had an erect and pleasing form, said unto the woman, "Yea, hath God said, Ye shall not eat of every tree of the garden? And the woman said unto the serpent, We may eat of the fruit of the trees of the garden: but of the fruit of the tree which is in the midst of the garden, God hath said, Ye shall not eat of it, neither shall ye touch it, lest ye die. And the serpent said unto the woman, Ye shall not surely die: for God doth know that in the day ye eat thereof, then your eyes shall be opened, and ye shall be as gods, knowing good and evil. And when the woman saw that the tree was good for food, and that it was pleasant to the eyes, and a tree to be desired to make one wise, she took of the fruit thereof, and did eat, and gave also unto her husband with her; and he did eat [Gen. 3:1-6].

Here the positive commandment of God was violated, the covenant of life broken, and the curse of death incurred, not only for himself, but for all his posterity. To explain philosophically how a perfectly holy creature could sin, is not easy, but as a practical matter the thing is not difficult. The mind of man was incapable of thinking of many things at once; to his constitution belong many natural desires and appetites. The objects suited to these might so occupy the mind, for a season, as to exclude higher and nobler ideas; and, in a moment of inadvertency the lower propensities, which act with a blind force, might prevail with persons, before innocent, to do an act which God had forbidden; especially, when by an impudent falsehood the danger of the act was positively denied, and when it was confidently alleged that great good would be the result.

Whether the man was influenced to eat by the same motives which prevailed with the woman is a matter of uncertainty. Many suppose that he was led by love to his wife to determine to perish with her, rather than be forever separated from her. It matters little what were his motives; the fact was that he deliberately transgressed the law of God, and thus involved a world in ruin.

The immediate consequences of the fatal transgression were a new set of feelings—guilt, shame, and fear

—which caused our first parents to cover themselves
with fig-leaves, and to hide themselves among the thick
trees of the garden. When questioned by their Maker,
they attempted to excuse themselves and to charge
their fault upon another. They were now driven from
the garden and flaming cherubim were stationed at the
entrance to prevent their return. The ground was
cursed for their sake and doomed thenceforth to bring
forth thorns and briars, so that man would have to eat
his bread by the sweat of his brow. The sentence of
death was also confirmed, "Dust thou art, and unto
dust shalt thou return" [Gen. 3:19]. It may be asked
how the threatening, "In the day that thou eatest thereof thou shalt surely die" [Gen. 2:17], was executed, since
Adam continued to live upon earth for more than nine
hundred years. "Let God be true, but every man a liar"
[Rom. 3:4]. This threatening was executed, or began to
be executed, that very day; for from the moment of
man's eating the forbidden fruit, he became mortal.
Death already began to work. In death, as threatened
in the penalty, every kind of evil is included. Temporal
death, consisting of a separation of soul and body, was
not the principal thing; but spiritual death, which consists in a separation from God, a loss of His favor and
image, and which perpetuated, is eternal death, commenced on the very day on which man sinned. While
man, after the fall, retained all his physical powers of
soul and body, and still continued to be a moral and
accountable creature, he entirely lost that clothing of
moral excellence which was the beauty and glory of his
nature. He was now dead in law, and dead in trespasses
and sins; and from being a holy being, became totally
depraved; that is, destitute of any principle of true

holiness, but capable of unlimited increase in wickedness.

That the posterity of Adam "sinned in him, and fell with him in his first transgression" is evident from the fact that they have all become mortal, and are subjected to all the temporal evils which fell upon him. They are all excluded from Paradise and are forced to till the earth with the sweat of their brow, which still groans under the curse, and spontaneously brings forth noxious weeds instead of useful grains and fruits. Woman is still, all over the world, subject to the same pains in parturition, which were threatened to Eve. But more than this, men come into the world destitute of that holiness, or original righteousness, in which Adam was created. By nature all are children of wrath. All go astray from their earliest years. "There is none that doeth good, no, not one." "The way of peace have they not known: There is no fear of God before their eyes" [Rom. 3:12, 17-18]. This state of corruption is not confined to idolatrous Gentiles, but belongs also to the Jews, who were in external covenant with God. "All have sinned, and come short of the glory of God" [Rom. 3:23]. And these streams of iniquity David traces up to the polluted fountain, when he cries out, "Behold, I was shapen in iniquity, and in sin did my mother conceive me" [Ps. 51:5].

That the universality of death in the human race is owing to the transgression of Adam is clearly evinced from the express declarations of Holy Scripture: "As in Adam all die, so in Christ shall all be made alive" [1 Cor. 15:22]. "As by one man sin entered into the world, and death by sin; so death hath passed on all men, for that (or in whom) all have sinned" [Rom. 5:12]; "For as by one man's disobedience many were made sinners" [Rom. 5:19]; "By one man's offence, death reigned by one" [Rom. 5:17]; "Through the offence of one many are dead." "By the offence of one judgment came upon all men to condemnation" [Rom. 5:18]. And the facts, known by universal experience, are in exact accord with these declarations of the Bible. All men die. That this is on account of the imputation of Adam's sin is evident because death reigns over "those who had not sinned after the similitude of Adam's transgression" [Rom. 5:14], that is, over infants who have not been guilty of any actual violation of the law of God.

Whether it was just in God to constitute Adam the representative of all his posterity and suspend their salvation on his obedience is not a question for us to discuss. Whatever God does is just, and not only just, but wise; though darkness may rest on this transaction, this is owing to our ignorance and prejudice. We need not fear that the Judge of all the earth will not be able to vindicate His own dispensations to the whole universe.

Some have thought to evade or lessen the apparent hardship of the case by denying the imputation of Adam's sin to his posterity, and maintaining that children were only punished for the depraved nature derived from Adam. But how did they come to inherit this depraved nature? Is not this the principal part of the curse? It goes only a little way to relieve the mind which labors to say that infants are punished for latent depravity, instead of suffering for the sin of Adam.

Instead of cavilling and complaining of the dispensations of the Almighty, by which we have become miserable sinners, let us not cease to bewail the deep corruption of our nature; and let us, instead of perplexing ourselves with fruitless inquiries about the principles of the divine government by which we have been involved in this ruin, earnestly seek to know what that gracious remedy is which God has provided for our recovery. The fact is certain that we are in a depraved and miserable state and unless we are redeemed from it we must be forever in a state of degradation and misery. When it is asserted that man is totally depraved, the meaning is not that he is as wicked as he is capable of being, or that all men are sinners in an equal degree; but that all men are by nature destitute of any principle of true holiness. All love the creature supremely and their carnal hearts are at enmity with God, and not subject unto His law, neither, indeed, can be. It is evident from what has been said that man is in a sinful, miserable, and helpless condition.

CHAPTER 17

Covenant of Grace, or Plan of Redemption

In this treatise the word "covenant" is used in a wide sense to correspond with the latitude which belongs to the original terms, of which this is a translation. Without attempting to give a very exact or logical definition of the phrase "covenant of grace," I would say that by it is meant the whole plan of redemption, from its commencement to its consummation; or, that gracious method of bestowing salvation on elect sinners which is revealed in the holy Scriptures.

The fall of man, by which God's chief work on earth was ruined, was not an unexpected event which took the omniscient God by surprise; nor could it disconcert that scheme which had been originally conceived in the eternal mind. "Known unto God are all his works from the beginning of the world" (Acts 15:18). Although God is not the author of sin and can never look upon evil but with the strongest disapprobation, yet, having created man a free, accountable creature, and having endowed him with full ability to obey the law under which he was placed, He chose to leave him to the freedom of his own will without exerting any direct influence on him, either to preserve him in obedience or to cause him to fall. Although He knew that man would fall into sin and ruin, yet He purposed to permit this, that is, to not hinder it, because He knew that He could make it the occasion of a more illustrious display of His attributes, especially of His justice and mercy, than could be made under other circumstances.

To have right views of the covenant of grace, it is essential to assume it as an undoubted truth that the condemnation of mankind under the covenant of works was just, and that the Ruler of the universe was not under any obligations to devise any plan of recovery for fallen man, any more than for fallen angels. If it would not have been just to leave men under the curse which they had incurred, then that covenant or law, under which man was placed, was not a righteous constitution; and if it would not have been just to leave the human race in the ruin in which they were involved, then their deliverance would not be a matter of grace, but of justice. A difference of opinion may exist among the orthodox as to the kind and degree of punishment to which the human race would have been subjected if the law had been executed fully upon them, but there can be but one opinion respecting the justice of their punishment by all who entertain correct opinions respecting the character and dispensations of the Governor of the universe. God was not bound to provide a Redeemer; this was a matter of mere grace and favor.

The origin of the covenant of grace was the unparalleled, incomprehensible love of God to sinners of the human race. The obstacles in the way of accomplishing the salvation of those whose death was demanded by law and justice were apparently insuperable. It may be presumed that if the problem how God could be just and yet justify the ungodly had been proposed to a conclave of the brightest angels in heaven, they could not have worked out a satisfactory answer; it would have baffled their utmost intellectual efforts. That God cannot cease to treat His creatures according to the principles of eternal justice is most evident; and that justice required that the sinner should suffer, according to his demerit, is equally evident. Where, then, is there any foundation for hope in regard to those who have once transgressed? And not only the justice, but the truth of God stood in the way of the sinner's salvation. God had threatened the penalty of death, interminable death; and the Ruler of the universe must maintain the truth of His word, as it respects His threatenings as well as His promises: "God is not a man that he should lie; nor the son of man, that he should repent" (Num. 29:13).

But that which could not be discovered by the wisdom of creatures was devised by the infinite wisdom of God. In the counsels of the adorable Trinity the plan was agreed upon. Between the Father and the Son, a transaction took place which may strictly be termed a covenant, for, speaking after the manner of men, there were mutual stipulations entered into between the high contracting parties. The Father, as Legislator and Governor of the universe, appoints the Son to the office of Mediator, and, on certain conditions, gives to Him a chosen people, elected from the common mass of fallen man, "according to the purpose of him who worketh all things after the counsel of his own will" [Eph. 1:11]. The Son willingly accepts the arduous office and engages to comply with the proposed conditions; and the Holy Spirit consents to perform His part in the execution and consummation of the glorious plan. But contriving and planning was not all that was requisite; the Mediator, in order to redeem man, must obey and suffer in his place, and this rendered it necessary that He should descend to earth and be born of a woman and made under the law. And this stoop of humiliation was not enough; the Son of God must suffer and die, in the room of the creature man. In order that He might exhaust the penalty due to man for sin, the Redeemer must not only die, but His death must be of the most bitter and accursed kind. To all this He consented and covenanted on behalf of His chosen, to meet all the demands of law and justice against them.

If any should ask what evidence we have of this covenant of redemption, we answer, in the words of the Mediator, "I appoint," or, as the original word imports, "I give by covenant, unto you, a kingdom, as the Father hath given by covenant unto me" (Luke 22:29). Again, "As thou hast given him power over all flesh, that he should give eternal life to as many as thou hast given him" (John 17:2). "I have manifested thy name unto the men which thou gavest me out of the world: thine they were and thou gavest them me" (John 17:6). "I pray for them: I pray not for the world, but for them which thou hast given me" (John 17:9). "Keep through thine own name those whom thou hast given me" [John 17:11]. And the solemn declaration in Psalm 89:3, "I have made a covenant with my chosen, I have sworn unto David my servant," has always, by the church, been referred to the Messiah, to the spiritual David, David's Lord and David's Son.

But why was this salvation confined to a certain favored number, called the elect of God? This doctrine of the sovereignty of divine grace, has, from the begin-

ning, been offensive to human reason. The selection of
men and not of angels, as the object of redemption, can
be borne with; but that, out of the same mass, some
should be taken, confessedly no better than others by
nature; and that many should be reprobated or left, no
worse than those elected, has ever been a stumbling-
block to multitudes. Hence, however plainly the doctrine
be revealed, they will not receive it, and frequently manifest great hostility to all who maintain and preach it, as
did the Jews when our Lord inculcated it by reference
to certain facts in the sacred history. But however offensive this doctrine is to human reason, since it is clearly
revealed and often expressed in the Word of God, we are
not at liberty to relinquish or conceal it. If God might
justly have left all men to perish in their sin, certainly
He may justly leave a part in that state of ruin into
which they have fallen. As all men are by nature children of wrath; the redemption of a part cannot alter or
affect the condition of the rest. Because the pardoning
power in the State releases certain persons from the
penalty of the law, this does not render it unjust to pun-
ish others who are under a sentence of condemnation.

The justice of God in this case is easily vindicated;
but it is not so easy to reconcile this proceeding with
His benevolence. If God could as easily have saved all
as a part, why did He not manifest His goodness in
doing so? To which it may be answered, that we do not
know the reasons of the divine conduct in this matter.
He, as an absolute Sovereign, has a right to do as seemeth good with His own. He constantly refers election to
His own good pleasure, to the counsel of His own will.
He has infinitely good reasons, but as He has not
revealed them, we have no right to inquire into them.

The manifestation of God's gracious purpose in the covenant of grace began to be made immediately after the fall; first, in the sentence pronounced on the serpent, in which it was declared that the seed of the woman should bruise the head of the serpent, that is, of "that old serpent, which is the Devil" [Rev. 20:2] and next by the institution of bloody sacrifices, and accepting the offerings of this kind made in faith, as in the case of Abel; and by various communications to the saints, until the time of Abraham, with whom God entered into a special covenant. To Abraham God made many gracious promises, and granted peculiar privileges to his descendants; He separated the chosen race from all the world, and placed the seal of His covenant in their flesh.

But when the seed of Jacob had grown to be a great nation in Egypt, where they were held in abject and cruel bondage, God appeared unto Moses at Mount Horeb in the burning bush and commissioned him to deliver His people, and by a series of wonderful miracles to conduct them to Canaan, which land He had promised to Abraham four hundred years before. While in the wilderness at the foot of Mount Sinai, God appeared in dreadful majesty to all the people, and uttered His holy law in ten commandments, in the midst of thunder and lightning and the sound of a trumpet, while the whole mountain burned with fire.

The moral law was binding on man by nature, but it had become so obliterated that it became necessary to republish it, that the people having the true standard of duty before them, might be convinced of their sins and driven to seek refuge in the atoning blood so copiously shed on the Jewish altar.

Besides the moral law, which was not only proclaimed by the voice of God but engraved by the finger
of God on two tables of stone, He gave many ritual
laws to be observed, instituted a priesthood and consecrated the family of Aaron to this service, and directed
Moses to erect a tabernacle for worship, exactly according to a pattern showed him on the mount, where he
remained in the presence of God forty days, without
eating or drinking, at two different times. All these
institutions of a ceremonial kind were intended to be
a shadow of good things to come.

This dispensation, administered by sacrifices, types,
and prophecies, continued without essential change until it was superseded by the more glorious dispensation
of the gospel, introduced after the advent of the Messiah; who being the Mediator of the new covenant, and
having answered all the types and fulfilled all the
prophecies, brought that dispensation to an end. The
New Testament dispensation, with clearer light, greater
liberty, more of the Spirit of adoption, and a spiritual
worship not confined to any particular place, nor bur-
dened with external forms and rites, it is believed, will
continue until the second advent of our Lord and Savior
Jesus Christ.

CHAPTER 18

The Incarnation

Christ did not come into the world until about four thousand years had elapsed from the creation. By this delay it clearly appeared how deep was the depravity of fallen man, as all nations, the Israelites only excepted, departed from God and lost the knowledge of His true character. And having apostatized from the worship and service of their Creator, they universally, with the exception already mentioned, addicted themselves to the most abominable idolatries, and to every species of degrading vice.

This apostasy was not owing to any defect of external light, for, as Paul teaches, "that which may be known of God is manifest in them; for God hath shewed it unto them. For the invisible things of him from the creation of the world are clearly seen, being understood by the things that are made, even his eternal power and Godhead; so that they are without excuse: because that, when they knew God, they glorified him not as God, neither were thankful; but became vain in their imaginations, and their foolish heart was darkened. Professing themselves to be wise, they became fools, and changed the glory of the incorruptible God into an image made like to corruptible man, and to birds, and four footed beasts, and creeping things" [Rom. 1:19-23].

It was proper that the world should have the opportunity of making trial of their own wisdom before the device of infinite wisdom should be manifested. Opportunity had also been thus afforded to prepare the way for the advent of the Mediator by a system of types and prophecies, which clearly designated His person and offices, and thus furnished indubitable evidence of His being indeed the Christ of God. The time selected for the advent of the Savior was also suitable, because the world was then full of inhabitants; the human mind had been highly cultivated, and the intellectual faculties had attained their utmost vigor, and all the civilized world were subject to one government; and the Latin and Greek languages were understood through the whole extent of the Roman empire. Although in the previous age civil discord and desolating wars disturbed the empire, all was now reduced to peace under Augustus Caesar, so that a favorable opportunity was afforded for propagating the gospel among the nations. Besides, the time of the Messiah's advent had been fixed in the distinct enunciations of prophecy. Shiloh was to come before the sceptre had entirely departed from Judah, which was now far on the wane. He was to fill the temple of Zerubbabel with His glory, which was soon after this destroyed. And the specified weeks of Daniel, when the Messiah should be cut off, were drawing to a close. The "fullness of time" was therefore come, when "God sent forth his Son, made of a woman, made under the law, to redeem them that were under the law" [Gal. 4:4].

It had been predicted in Isaiah 7:14, that "a virgin shall conceive, and bear a son, and shall call his name *Immanuel*," God with us. It was also foretold by the same prophet, that a child should be born, who should be "the mighty God" [Isa. 9:6]. There was, therefore, a general expectation among the Jews, that the advent of the Messiah was at hand; and this expectation was increased, when John the Baptist began to preach in the wilderness, saying, "the kingdom of heaven is at hand" [Matt. 3:2], thus fulfilling the prophecy of Isaiah: "The voice of him that crieth in the wilderness, Prepare ye the way of the Lord, make straight in the desert a highway for our God" (Isa. 40:3), and also the prediction of Malachi, "Behold, I will send my messenger, and he shall prepare the way before me," and again, "Behold, I will send you Elijah the prophet before the coming of the great and dreadful day of the Lord" (Mal. 3:1; Mal. 4:5).

The place of the Messiah's birth had been explicitly named by the prophet Micah; so that when the wise men from the east came to Jerusalem, and inquired where he was to be born who was King of the Jews, Herod the king called together a convention of all the priests and scribes to determine this question, which they appear to have agreed upon unanimously, for they immediately answered, "in Bethlehem of Judea" [Matt. 2:6], and referred to the prophecy of Micah. The providence of God in bringing about the fulfilment of this prophecy was remarkable, for Mary and her husband resided at Nazareth. But it had been so ordered by an imperial edict, that every person should resort to the town to which his family properly belonged, to be registered, with a view to a general taxation; and thus the mother of our Lord was brought to Bethlehem at the very time when she was to be delivered of the child, conceived in her womb by the power of the Holy Spirit. And as there was not found room for them in the inn, the Son of God was born in a stable, and laid in a manger.

This glorious event for our lost world was not suffered to take place without suitable notice; for however inattentive the great men of this world might be to this humble, but miraculous birth, the angels of God had their attention directed to it as the most important event which had ever occurred in our world. One of the heavenly host, probably Gabriel, appeared to a company of shepherds in the vicinity, who were watching their flocks by night, and said, "Behold, I bring you good tidings of great joy, which shall be to all people. For unto you is born this day in the city of David a Saviour, which is Christ the Lord" [Luke 2:10-11]. And as soon as he had delivered his message, "a multitude of the heavenly host" was with the angel, "praising God, and saying, Glory to God in the highest and on earth peace, good will toward men" [Luke 2:13-14].

Until Christ was about thirty years of age, He lived in retirement at Nazareth. When John, His forerunner, had been for some time engaged in his public ministry preaching repentance, and baptizing the people, Jesus came forth, and was baptized in the river Jordan. Having voluntarily placed Himself under the law, it was proper that He should comply with not only the moral precepts, but with all the ceremonial institutions then in force. For although He could not attend on these institutions as one who needed forgiveness, or purification, or repentance, yet as He came to take the sinner's place, He obeyed all the laws then obligatory on the people. In infancy, He was circumcised; when grown up, He attended the Jewish worship at the temple, partook of the passover, joined in the worship of the synagogue; as John was commissioned of God to preach and baptize, He submitted to his baptism. John at first forbade him, saying, "I have need to be baptized of thee, and comest thou to me?" [Matt. 3:14]. But Jesus answered, and said, "Suffer it to be so now" [Matt. 3:15], and assigned as a reason, "for thus it becometh us to fulfil all righteousness."

By the incarnation, the divine and human natures were mysteriously united. "The word was made flesh, and dwelt among us" [John 1:14]. "God was manifest in the flesh" [1 Tim. 3:16]. "Who, being in the form of God, thought it not robbery to be equal with God: but made himself of no reputation, and took upon him the form of a servant, and was made in the likeness of men: and being found in fashion as a man, he humbled himself, and became obedient unto death" [Phil. 2:6-8].

CHAPTER 19

The Expiatory Sufferings of Christ, or the Atonement

An atonement is that which expiates sin; which reconciles an offended party; which makes satisfaction for offences committed.

The reason why an atonement was necessary, was the inflexible nature of divine justice. This attribute leads the Ruler of the universe to render to every one his due; to treat every one according to his character. The justice of God was manifested in giving to man a righteous law, and annexing a penalty exactly proportioned to the demerit of every transgression. Such a penalty being annexed to the law, it is evident that to execute it is a righteous thing; and when this penalty is incurred by transgression, the Judge of all the earth, acting justly, must inflict it. He cannot deny Himself. "He is not a man that he should lie, or the son of man that he should repent" [Num. 23:19]. If the penalty of the law might be set aside in one instance, it might in all, and then government would be at an end. Indeed, no reason can be assigned for a difference; if one sinner is exempted from punishment, the same treatment should be extended to all; for, in the administration of law and justice, there should be uniformity, though that principle does not apply to the dispensation of grace.

How then can any sinner be saved? This is a problem which we are persuaded no finite intelligence could have solved. But what created wisdom could not discover, the wisdom of the triune God was able to accomplish. The principle of an adequate atonement by a qualified Surety was the one adopted. But who is sufficient to make the requisite satisfaction to law and justice? Upon the principles already stated, such a satisfaction was necessary. No mere creature could be the substitute; for, beside, that such an one would owe obedience for himself to the full extent of his powers, the actions and sufferings of a mere creature could not possess that merit which could be accepted, to answer the demands of the law against millions. Neither could any person of the Godhead perform the work of redemption. The Deity can neither suffer nor obey. This mighty difficulty can only be overcome by the constitution of a *person*, in whom both natures shall be united; that is, by the second person in the glorious Trinity assuming human nature into such intimate union with Himself, that the actions and sufferings of this nature shall be the actions and sufferings of the person of the Son of God. That such a substitution was admissible depended on the wisdom and will of God. Among men, there would exist strong reasons against permitting the innocent to die for the guilty; but when we inquire what these reasons are, we find that not one of them applies to the redemption of Christ. He has a complete right to dispose of Himself, and the power to qualify Himself for the arduous work. By admitting the substitution of Christ in the room of His chosen people, no injury is sustained in any quarter; for, though the Redeemer must endure an inconceivable weight of sorrow for a season, for this He will reap a glorious and endless reward. And though the guilty escape, yet the plan provides for their complete reformation; and the mercy of God is illustriously displayed, and placed in a light in which it never could have been, if this plan had not been revealed.

And not only is mercy and condescension exhibited in a bright and peculiar light, which gives to all the intelligent creation new discoveries of the divine character; but justice, which would have appeared glorious in the punishment of the guilty in exact proportion to their demerit, yet shines forth with a far brighter lustre in the sufferings of the only begotten Son of God than in the condign punishment of a world of guilty sinners. Here, then, we see what the nature of an atonement must be. It must remove those obstacles which stood in the way of the sinner's salvation. These arose from the law and justice of God, which demanded the life of the transgressor. The Redeemer, therefore, must make a full satisfaction to law and justice, or the sinner cannot be saved. He must render a meritorious obedience to the law which men had broken, and receive the punishment of their sins in His own person. The sufferings of Christ were, therefore, of a strictly vicarious nature. He "bare our sins in his own body on the tree" [1 Pet. 2:24]. He died, "the just for the unjust, that he might bring us to God" [1 Pet. 3:18]. "He was wounded for our transgressions, he was bruised for our iniquities" [Isa. 53:5]. "The LORD hath laid on him the iniquity of us all" [Isa. 53:6].

No doubt He set us a glorious example of perfect patience and fortitude, in enduring so much pain and ignominy; but example was not the main end of these sufferings, which would place them on the same level with those of other martyrs. And, it is not disputed that the death of Christ is calculated to produce a moral impression on all intelligent minds, but even this was not the direct end of Christ's sufferings, according to the Scriptures. He died as an expiatory victim, a sacrifice to satisfy divine justice, as atonement for all the sins of His chosen, as a ransom to redeem them from their bondage; yea, as a curse, to redeem them that were under the curse. This view of the atonement is vital to the Christian system. It is plainly the doctrine of the Old as well as the New Testament; it ever has been the doctrine of every sound part of the Christian church, and it would be easy to show that the objections to it are either frivolous, or they are such as subvert the gospel of Christ and bring in another gospel, which exposes the abettors of it to the anathema of Paul (Gal. 1:8).

All the sufferings of Christ should be considered as expiatory, and as constituting the atonement which He undertook to make for His people; and, indeed, His whole state of humiliation should be considered as belonging to His expiation. When He first felt the pangs incident to infancy, when He went about from day to day, "a man of sorrows, and acquainted with grief" [Isa. 53:3]; when reproached, slandered, and reviled; when hungry, thirsty, and weary; when filled with grief at the hardness and perverseness of the people, which drew tears from His eyes; when bathed in His own blood in Gethsemane; when betrayed, bound, dragged to trial; when falsely accused, and condemned; when mocked and reviled; when scourged, crowned with thorns, and fainting under the cross; when nailed to the tree and exposed to the profane gaze of the multitude denuded

of His garments; when exhausted with pain and thirst
—and above all, when forsaken of God—and when He
breathed out His soul in death, He was enduring the
penalty of the law. After He was taken from the cross
and laid in the sepulchre, though He suffered no positive pain, yet He was still bearing the curse or penalty
of the law, which was death. And if it be asked for
whom did the Redeemer bear all this, He has given the
answer, "I lay down my life for the sheep" [John 10:15].
He loved His church and gave Himself for it. But His
atonement, considered in its intrinsic value and suit-
ableness, is infinite, and sufficient if applied, to save the
whole world.

The sufferings of Christ, being those of a divine
person, have an infinite value; it follows, therefore,
that although the punishment of the sinner was
everlasting, yet Christ could exhaust the penalty of the
law in a limited time; that is, His sufferings and death,
though limited to a short period, were more than an
equivalent for the eternal sufferings of those for whom
He laid down His life. And in making this vicarious
atonement, it was not at all necessary that the Mediator should be the subject of remorse and despair; for
these are not essential to the penalty of the law, but
merely incidental, arising from the circumstances and
moral character of the sufferer. But it was necessary
that our substitute should suffer a painful and accursed death, for this was specifically threatened.
Some have supposed that Christ endured something of
the torments of the damned after His death, as the
creed says, "He descended into hell," but the word *hell*
here signifies no more than the place of departed
spirits, or the grave. Christ's sufferings were finished

on the cross; and on that very day His spirit entered into paradise (Luke 23:43). It cannot be reasonably doubted, but that all those for whom Christ offered Himself a sacrifice, will eventually be saved.

CHAPTER 20

Resurrection and Ascension of Christ

The blessed Redeemer, having been three days in the grave according to His own oft-repeated prediction (that is, a part of three days, which, according to the usual method of computing time, was reckoned for three days), rose from the dead, and during forty days, which He remained upon the earth, appeared a number of times to His disciples. He gave them not only ocular but palpable evidence of the reality of His resurrection. That there might remain no doubt of His identity, He showed them His hands and His feet, and even condescended to permit them to put their fingers into the print of the nails and to thrust their hands into the opening made in His side by a soldier's spear after His death. On one occasion, He appeared to above five hundred of His disciples convened on a mountain in Galilee, where He had promised before His crucifixion to meet them.

As the disciples had not understood His predictions respecting His death and resurrection, they were very slow to believe even their own senses. On this account, the risen Savior took pains to remove every shadow of doubt, and in several instances ate and drank in their presence, just as before His death. This time was also improved to give the apostles all needful instructions respecting their ministry after He should leave them.

At the expiration of the forty days, He led His disciples out to Mount Olivet, where He blessed them, was parted from them, and carried up to heaven in the midst of thousands of angels. The Holy Ghost says in Psalm 68:17-18 "The chariots of God are twenty thousand, even thousands of angels: the Lord is among them, as in Sinai, in the holy place. Thou hast ascended on high, thou hast led captivity captive: thou hast received gifts for men; yea, for the rebellious also, that the LORD God might dwell among them." Paul expressly applies this passage to Christ in Ephesians 4:8-9.

Until the time of His ascension, as far as appears, Christ's body remained the same as before His death; but as a body of flesh and blood, though free from every stain, is not suited to the heavenly state, it is reasonable to suppose that Christ's body now underwent a sudden change, such as we are informed will pass on the bodies of the saints who shall be found alive upon earth when Christ shall make His second appearance. Before His ascension, He had flesh and bones which could be handled and felt, but now He assumed that glorious body in which He appears in heaven, and in which every eye shall behold Him when He shall come in the clouds of heaven, with all His holy angels, to judge the world.

That Christ appeared after His resurrection in the same body which was nailed to the cross and laid in the sepulchre is as evident from the sacred Scriptures as words can make it. Luke gives the following explicit testimony: "Jesus himself stood in the midst of them, and saith unto them, Peace be unto you. But they were

terrified and affrighted, and supposed that they had
seen a spirit. And he said unto them, Why are ye
troubled? and why do thoughts arise in your hearts?
Behold my hands and my feet, that it is I myself; handle
me, and see; for a spirit hath not flesh and bones, as ye
see me have. And when he had thus spoken, he shewed
them his hands and his feet" [Luke 24:36-40]. Though
the fact is not mentioned, we may certainly infer that
Christ's body underwent a change before He entered
heaven; for we are assured that "flesh and blood
cannot inherit the kingdom of God" [1 Cor. 15:50], and
as this is true in regard to believers, it is equally so
respecting Christ. Still it is the same body that suffered
on the cross which is now in heaven at the right hand
of God—but now this body is glorified.

CHAPTER 21

Mediatorial Offices of Christ

The offices of Christ have long been divided into three: the prophetical, sacerdotal, and regal. This is not an arbitrary distinction, but is founded in the needs of men; for He who undertakes to save sinners must be qualified to deliver them from their ignorance, from their guilt, and from their depravity. He must have power to protect them from all their enemies, raise them from death and the grave, and bring them to the possession of eternal life.

When Christ was upon earth, most of His time during His public ministry was spent in teaching. In the exercise of this office, "He taught with authority, and not as the scribes" [Matt. 7:29; Mark 1:22]. Even in the judgment of His enemies, "never man spake like this man" [John 7:46]. But when about to leave the world, He promised to His disciples another teacher, who should remain with them and lead them into all truth, and who should bring to their remembrance whatever He had said to them. Thus, He now exercises the office of a prophet by His Word and Spirit, by which agency all the children of God are taught of Him; and through faith in the holy Scriptures, are made wise unto salvation. By the law they obtain the knowledge of sin; by the gospel they are made acquainted with the only remedy; and by the influence of the Holy Spirit they are enabled "to grow in grace, and in the knowledge of the Lord Jesus Christ" [2 Pet. 3:18].

As Moses prophesied that the Lord should raise up a prophet like unto him—that is, one who should be the author of a new dispensation—so, the same glorious person is predicted in the Psalms, as a priest, not after the order of Aaron, but after the order of Melchizedek: a priest who should have no predecessor nor successor, but should possess in Himself an everlasting priesthood, and who, by the sacrifice of Himself, should be able to accomplish what the levitical priests never could. What they performed and exhibited in shadows, He executed in substance. As their sacrifices and oblations were to remove ceremonial guilt and uncleanness, He, by the one offering of Himself, obtained eternal redemption for us. And as the high priest, on the great day of atonement, after slaying the sin-offering both for himself and the people, carried the blood into the most holy place and sprinkled it on the mercy seat, so Christ, the High Priest of our profession, having offered Himself as a sacrifice on the cross, has entered into the most holy place not made with hands, where He appears before God to present, as it were, the "blood which cleanseth from all sin" [1 John 1:7]. "For Christ is not entered into the holy places, made with hands, which are the figures of the true; but into heaven itself, now to appear in the presence of God for us." "For by one offering he hath perfected for ever them that are sanctified" (Heb. 9:24; Heb. 10:14).

Two things belong to the office of priesthood: first, oblation, or the offering a sacrifice; secondly, the sprinkling of the blood, or the presenting of the oblation before God. This, in Scripture, is called intercession because, on the ground of having complied with the stipulated conditions in the covenant of redemption, the Mediator has a right to claim the deliverance of those for whom He undertook. This, therefore, is a very necessary part of the mediatorial work. It is the moving cause of all that is done in the application of the purchased redemption. Therefore it is written "that he is able to save them to the uttermost that come unto God by him; seeing he ever liveth to make intercession for them" [Heb. 7:25].

Here we see the reason why the true believer never comes again into condemnation, notwithstanding all his sins and infirmities: he has an Advocate with the Father, who is the propitiation for his sins. As fast as he contracts guilt, his sins are blotted out; or, rather, as he has the righteousness of Christ set down to his account, he cannot come into condemnation. "If God be for us, who can be against us?" [Rom. 8:31], "Who shall lay any thing to the charge of God's elect? It is God that justifieth. Who is he that condemneth? It is Christ that died, yea rather, that is risen again, who is even at the right hand of God, who also maketh intercession for us" [Rom. 8:33-34]. The Christian then, in all his trials, under all his burdens, when tempted to despond or despair, should have recourse to the cross, and should look for comfort to the prevailing intercessions of his great High Priest.

In Psalm 2:6 it is written, "Yet have I set my king upon my holy hill of Zion." Jesus Christ was born a king. He was lineally descended from David, to whose family the regal authority was promised forever. When Pilate interrogated Him, whether He was a king, He did not deny it, but admitted and asserted it, saying, "Thou sayest that I am a king. To this end was I born, and for this cause came I into the world, that I should bear witness unto the truth" [John 18:37]. After His resurrection, He declared to His disciples, "all power is given unto me in heaven and in earth" [Matt. 28:18]. And we read "that angels and principalities are subject to him" [1 Pet. 3:22]. He is made "head over all things for his church, which is his body" [cf. Eph. 1:22; Col. 1:18]. He is therefore called "the King of kings and Lord of lords" [1 Tim. 6:15; Rev. 19:16]. "For he must reign until he hath put all enemies under his feet" [1 Cor. 15:25].

In the exercise of His regal office, He governs all providential events and revolutions so as to promote the ultimate glory and triumph of His kingdom. He holds under restraint all those enemies who would otherwise destroy His sheep. Over these He watches with a shepherd's care. In the exercise of His regal office He will judge the world in righteousness. "We shall all stand before the judgment seat of Christ" [cf. Rom. 14:10; 2 Cor. 5:10]. "When the Son of man shall come in his glory, and all the holy angels with him, then shall he sit upon the throne of his glory. Then shall the King say unto them on his right hand, Come, ye blessed of my Father, inherit the kingdom prepared for you from the foundation of the world" [Matt. 25:31, 34].

CHAPTER 22

Justification

Correct ideas on the subject of a sinner's justification are exceedingly important because this is a cardinal point in the Christian system. A mistake here will be apt to extend its pernicious influence to every other important doctrine. There is in human nature a strong tendency to build on a false foundation. For man, when created, was placed under a covenant of works; and, by nature, he knows no other way than "do and live." Human reason and the dictates of conscience urge men to seek the favor of God by obeying His will. If we were able to render to the law such an obedience as would secure justification, this would still be the right way and no other need be sought. "If there had been a law," says Paul, "which could have given life, verily righteousness (or justification) should have been by the law" [Gal. 3:21]. "For what the law could not do, in that it was weak through the flesh, God sending his own Son in the likeness of sinful flesh, and for sin, condemned sin in the flesh: that the righteousness of the law might be fulfilled in us, who walk not after the flesh, but after the Spirit" [Rom. 8:3-4].

In most cases we should think it unnecessary and inexpedient to contend about the meaning of a word when they who used it explained the sense in which they take it, but here it is exceedingly important to ascertain

the scriptural meaning of the word *justification*, for
this is the point from which men's opinions are most
apt to diverge from the dictates of divine revelation. If
we put a wrong sense on the word, it will be sure to
favor the dangerous doctrine of human merit.

We would, therefore, lay it down as a truth capable
of the clearest proof that justification, as used in Scripture, does not mean any change wrought within us,
but a change of our relation or standing under the law.
As condemnation does not signify the making a man
wicked, but declaring him guilty; so justification, which
is the very opposite of condemnation, does not mean
the infusion of holiness or justice into the hearts of
men, but it is the sentence of a judge declaring that the
person to whom it appertains is acquitted from every
charge and stands right in the view of the law. It is then
the act of the Judge of the universe, by which it is
declared, that all condemnation is removed, and that the
sinful man is accepted as righteous in the eye of the law.
It is evident that there can be no justification by any law
unless the person accused can plead a perfect righteousness; for if he has sinned but once, that one sin will
prevent his justification as certainly as a thousand. After
Adam had committed the first sin, it was impossible he
should ever be justified by his own works.

This is also the way the word is used in regard to
human laws. If a man is arraigned before any just tribunal and it is proved that he has committed one
felonious act, the judge cannot justify him. Hence it appears evident to reason, and the same thing is
repeatedly and emphatically taught in Scripture, "that
no man is justified by the law in the sight of God"
[Rom. 3:20; Gal. 3:11]. And the reason simply is, that

no man's obedience to the law is perfect. The idea entertained by some that a sinner's imperfect obedience may be the ground of justification is, therefore, evidently absurd. And the opinion that the moral law is changed, and so relaxed as to be level to the capacity of sinful creatures, is false and unscriptural, and tends to introduce another gospel, entirely subversive of the true system of salvation. Man's sincere obedience, though imperfect, may be an evidence that he is in a justified state, but never can be the ground of the sentence of the Judge.

The question then returns, "How can any man be just with God, since 'all have sinned and come short of the glory of God'?" [Rom. 3:23]. To which we answer, that a man under the gospel is justified by faith, without the deeds of the law; that is, he is justified by the perfect righteousness of Christ, received by faith. This righteousness is imputed to the believing sinner; that is, God treats him as if he himself had wrought it out.

God, the Judge, views the sinner, considered in his own character, chargeable with innumerable transgressions of His holy law; but when this ungodly man truly believes and becomes united to Christ, He imputes to him the perfect righteousness of His Surety, who has, in his stead, obeyed the precept and suffered the penalty of the law; and thus rendered a complete satisfaction to both law and justice. He can, therefore, be just while He justifies the ungodly; for the sentence is not pronounced on the ground of any righteousness which the believing sinner has of his own, but entirely on the ground of the perfect righteousness of the Mediator, which is accepted as though it had been rendered by himself. In this transaction there is no erroneous judgment; for the Judge sees everything as it is, and pardons the sinner and accepts his person, because he is viewed, "not having [his] own righteousness, which is of the law, but that which is through the faith of Christ, the righteousness which is of God by faith" [Phil. 3:9].

Some are willing to admit that the forgiveness of sin is on account of the atonement of Christ, but they are strongly opposed to the idea that Christ's actual obedience to the law should be the ground of the believer's being adjudged to eternal life. But if this be excluded, then the believer's own obedience must be the ground on which he receives life. Here again its imperfection renders it impossible that it should entitle him to any reward, much less to the reward of eternal life. The Scriptures, however, settle this dispute. Paul says, "As by one man's disobedience many were made sinners, so by the obedience of one shall many be made righteous" [Rom. 5:19]. Christ is, by the prophet, emphatically called, *"The Lord our righteousness"* [Jer. 23:6].

This is charged upon the Jews as their fatal mistake, "for they being ignorant of God's righteousness, and going about to establish their own righteousness, have not submitted themselves unto the righteousness of God" [Rom. 10:3]. It is then declared that "Christ is the end of the law for righteousness to every one that believeth" [Rom. 10:4].

As it is said that faith is "imputed...for righteousness" [James 2:23], many have adopted the opinion that the act of faith is graciously accepted, instead of a legal righteousness. But this would be inconsistent with the scope of the apostle whose main object is to show that justification is entirely gratuitous on account of Christ's merit; but faith is as much our act and our work, as anything else. If, therefore, a man is justified by his own faith, then boasting is no more excluded, than when he seeks justification by many good acts. Besides, the Judge of all cannot declare that the mere act of faith answers all the demands of the law. Therefore, when it is said that faith is imputed for righteousness, it must relate to the object of faith, even the perfect righteousness of Christ. If a condemned criminal should be pardoned by his prince on account of the intercession of his own son, when the pardon is offered, the man gladly accepts it. This act of acceptance may be said to save him from death, but the true ground of his deliverance is the intercession of the prince. In this way, as a mere instrument, faith justifies the sinner, and is imputed for righteousness, because it lays hold of and appropriates the righteousness of God by which the law of God has been completely satisfied.

Others, considering faith as the root of every Christian virtue and the spring of all good works, adopt the opinion that to be justified by faith is the same as to be justified by our whole evangelical obedience, and that the works excluded by Paul, are either ceremonial observances, or "dead works" [*cf.* Heb. 6:1; Heb. 9:14], not proceeding from faith. To this theory the same objection lies, as has been already urged; namely, that this righteousness is imperfect, and no imperfect righteousness can justify. Another objection which is fatal to this theory is that the sinner is justified completely when he first believes: "There is therefore now no condemnation to them which are in Christ Jesus" [Rom. 8:1], "being justified freely by his grace" [Rom. 3:24], "being justified by faith" [Rom. 5:1]. But if evangelical obedience is the ground of justification, no man can be justified in this life, for he will be engaged in working out this righteousness all his life. This consequence being inevitable, a learned commentator maintains that there is no justification until the day of judgment.

There is nothing more difficult than to bring men off from dependence, in some form, on their own righteousness. Therefore, the advocates of human merit and justification by works have seized with avidity upon the words of the apostle James, who declares that "by works a man is justified, and not by faith only" [James 2:24]. If he used the words "faith" and "justification" in the same sense as that in which they are used by Paul, there would be a flat contradiction between these two apostles. Thus Luther viewed the matter, at first, and, therefore, for a while, rejected the epistle of James.

But when the scope of this apostle is considered and the whole discourse impartially weighed, it will be found that he and Paul did not disagree in doctrine, though they employ the terms mentioned in a somewhat different sense. James was engaged in refuting the opinion of certain professors who held that all that was necessary to justification was a speculative assent to the truth. He shows that such a faith, being dead, could not justify. His doctrine is that a living, operative faith is necessary; and that our faith must be shown by our works, which is the same thing that Paul taught. Moreover, he uses the word justification in the passage referred to, not for a sinner's acceptance with God, at first, but that which showed his sincerity: those good works which the saints perform justify them in the eyes of men. This is evident from the example of Abraham, for he asks, Was not Abraham justified by works, when he offered up his son? But the pious act of offering up Isaac took place many years after God had accepted Abraham, and entered into covenant with him. This act, therefore, could not have been the ground of his justification in the sight of God; but it justified the sincerity of his profession, and showed that he was indeed a true believer. These apostles, therefore, do not differ, but essentially agree in their doctrine.

By an impartial consideration of all the schemes of justification which have been devised, there is none which gives due honor to the divine law, except that which represents the righteousness of Christ imputed and received by faith, as the only ground of a sinner's pardon and acceptance. If God could have been just while justifying the sinner on any other ground, the whole mediatorial work of Christ might have been dispensed with.

A common objection to this doctrine of gratuitous justification is that it tends to negligence and licentiousness. This objection is as old as the time of Paul, for he states it distinctly and answers it effectually. "Do we then make void the law through faith? God forbid: yea, we establish the law" [Rom. 3:31]. "Shall we continue in sin, that grace may abound? God forbid. How shall we, that are dead to sin, live any longer therein?" [Rom. 6:1-2]. The faith which justifies, works by love and purifies the heart; therefore, the justified person cannot be negligent of good works. If an appeal be made to facts, it will be found that those who maintain this doctrine are not deficient in obedience, on a comparison with those who hold a different doctrine.

CHAPTER 23

Regeneration and Conversion

The necessity of a change of moral character in man arises from the fact that by nature all men are "dead in trespasses and sins" [Eph. 2:1], and therefore, if any of the human race are ever saved, they must be regenerated. Even if a man could be justified and yet remain under the power of sin, he could not be happy, because sin contains in itself the seeds of misery, and such a one would certainly be incapable of participating in the joys of heaven, which require a holy nature to perceive or relish them. Therefore, our Lord said to Nicodemus, "except a man be born again, he cannot see the kingdom of God" [John 3:3].

It is not necessary to be very exact in distinguishing between regeneration and conversion, especially as the Scriptures appear to speak of both together. But it may not be amiss to remark that regeneration, which is the communication of spiritual life, is the act of God; conversion, which is a turning from sin to God, is our act, in consequence of the divine influence exerted on our minds.

That God is the author of regeneration is evident from Scripture and from the nature of the case. The same power that caused light to shine out of darkness must shine into our hearts to give us the light of the knowledge of God. "Which were born, not of blood, nor of the will of the flesh, nor of the will of man, but of God" [John 1:13]. As this work in the economy of salvation belongs to the Holy Spirit, it is said, "Except a man be born of water and of the Spirit, he cannot enter into the kingdom of God" [John 3:5]. That man cannot regenerate himself is too evident to need a remark. Life, in all cases, is the gift of God. If spiritual life be extinct in man, none but the power of God is adequate to rekindle it. It would be as reasonable to suppose that the human body, when deprived of animal life, could restore itself to activity and animation, as that a soul dead in sin should be able to perform the acts which appertain to spiritual life.

It is said that we are "born again...by the word of God, which liveth and abideth for ever" [1 Pet. 1:23], and that God, of His own will, "begat...us with the word of truth" [James 1:18]. But the Word, in this case, must be considered as an instrument in the hands of the Spirit; it can have no saving efficacy without a divine energy accompanying it. But how is the Word a means of regeneration? To this two answers may be given, accordingly as we use the word regeneration in a stricter or wider sense. As the operation of God in the communication of life to the soul is an instantaneous act, there is no place for any instrumentality in producing the effect; and as the Word only produces a saving effect, when the heart is prepared by grace, the Word is the means of regeneration only as God has connected the influences of the Spirit with the preaching and reading of the Word. But if we take the new birth in a wider sense, to include not merely the operation of God on the soul but also the effects produced in the changed views and feelings of the soul, then we can easily understand how the Word is a means of giving knowledge to the mind, and of exciting those exercises and affections in which the spiritual life essentially consists. The Word alone can never generate a true faith; but, when the Spirit of God has operated on the blind mind, the glorious truths of the gospel begin to appear in their true light and become the object of a saving faith. So also, when the beauty of holiness is perceived by means of the Word, love is excited; and when sin is viewed as exhibited in the Word of God as odious and abominable, true repentance is enkindled; and thus of every other exercise of the renewed nature. It may, therefore, be truly said that in every act of the spiritual life, the Word of truth is concerned; it presents the proper object and supplies the persuasive motive. Indeed, if the mind were in a state free from blindness and corruption, the mere objective presentation of the truth, without any supernatural influences, would bring into exercise all holy acts and affections.

In regeneration there is no new faculty created, understanding by the word *faculty* some constituent power of the soul; for as by the fall man did not cease to be a moral agent, but retained all the faculties which belonged to him as man, so in regeneration no new faculty is produced. The loss was not of any physical power, but of the moral excellence in which man was created. The same soul may be in ignorance, or filled with knowledge; it may be actuated by holy desires and affections, or the contrary. The moral character is a kind of clothing of the soul which may be essentially changed, while the essence of the soul and its natural faculties remain unchanged.

Although almighty power is exerted in the regeneration of a sinner, yet man is only conscious of the effects as they appear in the exercises of the renewed mind. As the end accomplished in this change is the partial restoration of the lost image of God, or "knowledge" and "true holiness," the evidences of regeneration are the same as the evidences of a holy nature. And as spiritual or holy exercises are specifically different from all others, there would be no difficulty in discerning the characteristics of piety in ourselves, were it not for the feebleness of these exercises and the sad mixture of feelings of an opposite nature.

The best way, therefore, to obtain a comfortable assurance that we are regenerated, is to press on with assiduity and alacrity in the divine life. That which is obscure in itself will not become clear by poring over it ever so long; but if we emerge from our darkness and come forth into the light, we shall be able to discern clearly what was before involved in obscurity. If we would know whether our faith and love and hope are genuine, we must seek to bring these graces into lively exercise, and then we cannot avoid perceiving their true character. But as faith is really the apprehension and reception of offered mercy, it is by directly believing in Christ, or actually rolling our burdens on Him, that we experience peace and confidence. Where a good work is begun, it will be carried on. None but they who persevere to the end shall be saved.

In concluding this chapter, we may adopt the language of the beloved disciple, "Behold, what manner of love the Father hath bestowed upon us, that we should be called the sons of God.... Beloved, now are we the sons of God, and it doth not yet appear what we shall be: but we know that, when he shall appear, we shall be like him; for we shall see him as he is" [1 John 3:1, 2].

CHAPTER 24

Repentance Toward God and Faith in our Lord Jesus Christ

Paul gives "repentance toward God and faith toward our Lord Jesus Christ" [Acts 20:21] as a summary of his preaching, during his two years' ministry at Ephesus. This comprehends the whole counsel of God, and includes whatever was profitable to the people.

Repentance literally signifies a change of mind for the better. In our Shorter Catechism, it is defined as "a saving grace, whereby a sinner out of a true sense of his sin, and apprehension of the mercy of God in Christ, doth, with grief and hatred of his sin, turn from it unto God, with full purpose of and endeavour after new obedience" [SC 87]. In the same place, faith is defined as "a saving grace, whereby we receive and rest upon him (Jesus Christ) for salvation as he is freely offered in the gospel" [SC 86]. Whatever difference of opinion there may be as to the precise meaning of these scriptural terms, all sound Christians will admit that for popular and practical use no language could be selected which would more perspicuously and properly convey to the reader a true notion of these fundamental graces. As to the precedence of one before the other, it is a question as impertinent as whether a whole precedes one of its parts, or is preceded by it. No man can give a sound definition of evangelical repentance which will not include faith. But if the word repentance be used in a more restricted sense, for godly sorrow for sin and hatred of it, it must be preceded by a true faith, for seeing in a rational mind goes before feeling. There must be a perception of the holiness of the divine law, before the turpitude of sin can be so seen as to occasion hatred of it and grief on account of it. But if by faith be meant that cordial reception of Christ, which is mentioned in the words cited from the Catechism, then certainly, there must be some true sense of sin before we can appreciate Christ as a Savior from sin. But it is altogether wrong to perplex the minds of serious Christians with useless questions of this sort. Let the schoolmen discuss such matters to their heart's content, but let the humble Christian rest in the plain and obvious meaning of the words of Scripture. The effect of divine truth on the heart is produced by general views, and not by nice and metaphysical distinctions.

Both faith and repentance must be proved to be genuine by their fruits. "Faith...worketh by love" [Gal. 5:6] and purifies the heart. "This is the victory that overcometh the world, even our faith" [1 John 5:4]. James says, "Show me thy faith without thy works, and I will show thee my faith by my works" [James 2:18]. Repentance is itself a turning from sin unto God. It is the commencement of a reformation from all sin. John the Baptist, when he inculcated repentance, at the same time called upon the people "to bring forth fruits meet for repentance" [Matt. 3:8]. Repentance is no atonement for sin but it is indissolubly connected with the pardon of sin. Therefore it was said, "Repent...and be converted, that your sins may be blotted out" [Acts 3:19].

CHAPTER 25

Sanctification, or Growth in Grace

In regeneration, spiritual life is communicated; but this incipient principle is in its infancy when first implanted. The vigor of spiritual life seems to be analogous to natural life, very different in different subjects. But in all it is imperfect and needs to be assiduously cherished and nurtured, that it may daily gain strength, and gradually rise to maturity. There are various means of divine appointment conducive to this end, in the use of which growth is as certain as in the body when supplied with nutriment. In the former as well as in the latter, there may be seasons of decay, arising from various untoward causes; but it may be assumed as a fact that where the principle of piety is really radicated in the soul, there will be growth; the steady tendency will be to a state of maturity. Although perfection is never attained in this life, yet there is in all true Christians a sincere desire after it and there may be a constant approximation toward it, as long as they live. Such a state of piety may be attained, as, comparatively, may be termed a state of perfection, and is so termed in Scripture. From what has been said it will be apparent that sanctification does not differ specifically from regeneration; the one is the commencement, the other the continuance and increase of the same principle.

Two things are commonly intended by the word

sanctification. The first is the mortification of sin; the last, the increase of the vigor and constancy of the exercises of piety. Although these may be distinguished, yet there is no need to treat them separately, because the advancement of the one cannot but be accompanied with progress in the other. Like the two scales of a balance, when one is depressed the other rises, so in the divine life in the soul, if pride is humbled, humility is of necessity increased; if the undue love of the creature is mortified, the love of God will be strengthened; and so of every other grace. Indeed, when we examine the subject accurately, we shall find that all real mortification of sin is by the exercise of faith, and those holy affections which flow from it. By legal striving, however earnest, or by ascetic discipline, however rigid, very little headway is made against the stream of inherent corruption. It is right, indeed, to keep the body under, lest its blind appetites and impulses should hinder the exercises of religion; and occasional fasting, when free from superstition, does greatly aid the spiritual progress of the true Christian. This is especially the fact when he is in conflict with some fleshly lust, or easily besetting sin. A pampered body will ever be an enemy to growth in grace.

It must not be forgotten that we are as dependent on the Holy Spirit for every holy act and exercise as for the ability to put forth the first act of faith, when regenerated. We have no strength in ourselves, in consequence of our justification and conversion. Christ has said, "Without me ye can do nothing" [John 15:5]. He is the vine, and believers are the branches. "As the branch cannot bear fruit of itself, except it abide in the vine; no more can ye, except ye abide in me" [John

15:4]. Yet this does not take away or diminish our motives for exertion; so far from it, that it affords the only encouragement which we have for diligence in the use of means. For though the power is of God, that power is exerted through the means of divine appointment. Therefore, in Scripture, divine aid and human agency are constantly united. When Christians are exhorted "to work out your own salvation" [Phil. 2:12], the reason assigned is, "for it is God which worketh in you both to will and to do of his good pleasure" [Phil. 2:13].

Where two opposite principles exist in the same person, there must be a conflict. When the whole current of the affections runs toward the world, there being no opposing principle, no conflict is experienced, except that which arises from the remonstrances of conscience; or from the discordant craving of conflicting desires of a sinful kind. But in the true believer, "the flesh lusteth against the Spirit, and the Spirit against the flesh: and these are contrary the one to the other: so that ye cannot do the things that ye would" [Gal. 5:17]. And often the spiritual man is made to groan in agony, and to cry out, "O wretched man that I am! who shall deliver me from the body of this death?" [Rom. 7:24]. Although in this warfare the principle of grace is generally victorious, for it is written, "sin shall not have dominion over you" [Rom. 6:14], yet, sometimes, by the power of temptation, and negligence in watchfulness, the man of God is cast down and degraded, and unless raised up by the hand of the Captain of his salvation, he would rise no more. But as the work of grace was begun without any merit or cooperation of the believer, the same love which at first effectually called him away from his sins and from the world, still pursues him, and will not suffer the enemy ultimately to triumph over him. Satan shall never have the opportunity of boasting that he has accomplished the ruin of one whom God purposed to save through Christ's death and who has been effectually called by the Holy Spirit. He may fall, but he shall rise again, for God hath said, "My grace is sufficient for thee" [2 Cor. 12:9], and, "I will never leave thee nor forsake thee" [Heb. 13:5]. Not unfrequently, the very falls of the children of God are overruled for their more rapid progress in the future. Nothing more tends to humble the soul and destroy self-confidence than being overtaken by such faults.

The means of sanctification may be comprehended under two general heads: the Word of God and prayer. The first is the food which is provided for the nourishment of the soul and by which it lives. Christ himself is indeed the bread of life—the manna that came down from heaven; but it is only in the Word, that we can find Christ; there He is revealed—there His dignity and glory are manifested—there we behold His holy life, miracles, sufferings, death, resurrection, ascension, and intercession. The whole object of faith, love, and hope is found in the Word of God. Therefore, it is by the assiduous study of the Word, and meditation on its truths, that we are to expect an increase of faith and a real growth in grace.

The other principal means of growth is prayer; especially, prayer for the influences of the Holy Spirit. Without the Spirit, as we have seen, there can be no progress; but this sum of blessings is graciously promised in answer to prayer. And these two means are harmonious; for the Word is the "sword of the Spirit"

[Eph. 6:17]. The Spirit operates only by the Word. Therefore, though we read that sanctification is of the Spirit, we also read that effectual prayer of Jesus Christ, "Sanctify them through thy truth: thy word is truth" [John 17:17].

Although all the means of sanctification may be comprehended under the Word of God and prayer, yet there are many subordinate means, which have a powerful efficacy in giving application and force to these. In this light may be considered the ministry, the reading of good books, attendance on the sacraments, and fasting. There is one means of grace of this class which we are not required to resort to, but which is often employed by our heavenly Father with great effect, in promoting the sanctification of His children: the chastisements of His rod. The benefit of affliction is often celebrated in Scripture; and almost every child of God can, after a few years' experience, adopt the language of the royal Psalmist, and say, "It is good for me that I have been afflicted" [Ps. 119:71]. Paul testifies, that though "no chastisement for the present seemeth to be joyous, but grievous: nevertheless afterwards it yieldeth the peaceable fruit of righteousness unto them which are exercised thereby" [Heb. 12:11]. Afflictions are often used as the means of recovering the children of God from a state of backsliding; as says David, "Before I was afflicted I went astray: but now have I kept thy word" [Ps. 119:67].

Though Christians do not arrive at sinless perfection in this life, yet it is a state to which every humble child of God shall attain at death. Christ will present His whole body before His Father's throne, "without spot, or wrinkle, or any such thing" [Eph. 5:27]. "We shall be like him; for we shall see him as he is" [1 John 3:2].

CHAPTER 26

Good Works, or Christian Duties

"Truth is in order to goodness," and the great touchstone of truth is its tendency to promote holiness. According to the Savior's rule, "By their fruits ye shall know them" [Matt. 7:20].

Good works are such as the law of God requires to be performed by all persons, according to the relations in which they stand, and the positive precepts which He has enjoined, and which are in force at the time. They have been commonly divided into three classes: the duties which we owe to God, to our neighbor, and to ourselves; but in strict propriety of speech, all our duties, whoever may be the object, are due to God. He is our Lawgiver, and we are under the moral government of no other.

Though Christ fulfilled the preceptive part of the law in the room of God's chosen people, yet He did not thereby free them from the obligation of obedience to the moral law. Such a release from moral obligation is inconceivable; for it is impossible that a creature should not be under obligations to love and honor his Creator; but if such exemption from law were possible, it would be no blessing but a curse; for our happiness consists in conformity to the law of God. "In keeping [thy commandments] there is great reward" [Ps. 19:11].

As the obligation to obedience cannot be removed,

so neither can the requisitions of the law, as some suppose, be lowered. Man must ever be as much bound to love God with the whole heart, as to love Him at all. If man had fulfilled the condition of the first covenant, which required perfect obedience during his probation, he would not have been free from moral obligation to obedience, in consequence of his justification. Angels, who are supposed to be now confirmed in happiness, are as much under obligation to love God as ever. Indeed, as has been hinted, holiness and happiness are inseparable. The Holy Scriptures abound in exhortations to Christians to be diligent, zealous, and persevering in the performance of the respective duties of their stations; in the performance of which, divine aid may be asked and confidently expected.

Some duties are incumbent on all classes of people, such as the worship of God, doing good to men, and abstaining from everything which would have a tendency to dishonor Christ, to injure our neighbor, or hinder our own usefulness and improvement. Two things especially are incumbent on all, in relation to their fellow-creatures residing on the earth with them. The first is the communication of saving knowledge to such as are so unfortunate as to be destitute of this precious treasure. This is a duty of universal obligation, though the means proper to be used by different persons will vary, according to the variety of the circumstances in which they are placed. It is the duty of all Christians to "let your speech be alway with grace, seasoned with salt, that ye may know how ye ought to answer every man" [Col. 4:6]. It is also their duty to exhort and admonish one another daily, lest any be hardened through the deceitfulness of sin. All Christians are bound also to teach by example as well as by precept, by exhibiting to the view of all who see them a holy life. "Let," says Paul, "your conversation be as it becometh the gospel" [Phil. 1:27]. And our blessed Lord in His Sermon on the Mount, commands: "Let your light so shine before men, that they may see your good works, and glorify your Father which is in heaven" [Matt. 5:16]. It is evident from the very nature of this duty, which arises from our obligation to love our neighbor as ourselves, that all Christians are bound to send the gospel to those who are destitute of this necessary means of salvation; for, "how shall they hear without a preacher? And how shall they preach, except they be sent?" [Rom. 10:14-15]. All, therefore, according to their ability, should contribute toward this object by supporting missionaries, aiding in the printing and circulation of Bibles and evangelical tracts, and maintaining institutions of learning for the training of ministers. But this duty of diffusing abroad the precious seed of divine truth, devolves especially on those who have been called to the holy ministry, who have been ordained for this very purpose, to publish to every creature the gospel of the grace of God. When a dispensation of the gospel is committed to any one, he will incur a fearful load of guilt if he turn aside to any secular employment. This may be learned from many things left on record by the apostle Paul. He calls God to witness that he was free from the blood of all men at Ephesus, because he had not ceased to declare unto them repentance toward God and faith in our Lord Jesus Christ; evidently intimating that if he had not been thus faithful and diligent, he would have incurred the guilt of their destruction; which is exactly in accordance with what is said respecting the unfaithful watchman in Ezekiel 33:1-9. The duty of preaching to those who are called and have undertaken the office, is not optional. This is evident from what Paul says in 1 Corinthians 9:16, "Woe is unto me, if I preach not the gospel!"

Others, who have the instruction of youth committed to them, are under peculiar obligations to instill into their opening minds the doctrines of God's holy Word. Parents, guardians of orphans, masters of servants or apprentices, and teachers of schools of every kind are bound by this obligation, from which no human laws can exempt them.

Another duty of universal obligation is to pray to God for His blessing on all the nations of the earth, and especially on kings and all that are in authority, not only that they may obtain salvation, but that Christians under a wise and equitable administration of law, "may lead a quiet and peaceable life in all godliness and honesty" [1 Tim. 2:2]. All are bound to join cordially and fervently in the public prayers of the church, and not to neglect the assembling themselves together, as the manner of some is. We have encouragement also to agree together in smaller associations for prayer; and are assured that Christ will be present in such meetings, and that the concordant prayers there offered will be graciously answered. And who can doubt, that, as we are commanded "to pray without ceasing" [1 Thess. 5:17], and to "pray every where, lifting up holy hands" [1 Tim. 2:8], family prayer is an incumbent duty? But in addition to all these, "enter into thy closet, and when thou hast shut thy door, pray to thy Father which is in secret; and thy Father which seeth in secret shall reward thee openly" [Matt. 6:6].

Among the prescribed duties of Christians, there is none which is more solemnly and emphatically inculcated than a compassionate regard to the poor and afflicted. Indeed, the phrase "good works" is most commonly employed in Scripture in relation to this single thing. In this we follow the example of Christ, "who went about doing good" [Acts 10:38], by preaching the gospel to the poor and by relieving the distresses of the afflicted.

It is the assiduous performance of this duty which recommends the gospel to the judgment and conscience of men, more than anything else. "Pure religion and undefiled before God and the Father is this, To visit the fatherless and widows in their affliction, and to keep himself unspotted from the world" [James 1:27]. Nothing more is necessary to convince us of the importance of this duty than the representation given by our Savior of the process of the judgment recorded in Matthew 25, where the destiny of the assembled race of men is made to turn upon the kindness shown to the disciples of Christ. "Then shall the King say unto them on his right hand, Come, ye blessed of my Father, inherit the kingdom prepared for you from the foundation of the world: for I was an hungered, and ye gave me meat: I was thirsty, and ye gave me drink: I was a stranger, and ye took me in: naked, and ye clothed me: I was sick, and ye visited me: I was in prison, and ye came unto me" [Matt. 25:34-36]. In answer to their inquiry, When they had done any of these things to Him? He said, "Inasmuch as ye have done it unto one of the least of these my brethren, ye have done it unto me" [Matt. 25:40]. And to the wicked, only the neglect of this duty is mentioned as the ground of condemnation.

Among the good works Christians are required to perform, relative duties hold a very conspicuous place. These, indeed, in number, greatly exceed all other Christian duties, and no day passes in which every one has not duties of this kind to perform. But, as the relations of men are very much diversified by their condition in life and standing in society, these duties are not the same to all persons. One is a parent, another a child; one is a magistrate, another a citizen; one is a pastor, another a member of his flock; one is a master, another a servant; one is a husband, another a wife. Besides these, there are particular professions and occupations in life, or offices in the church and state, all which relations give rise to duties that are incumbent on all who sustain these various relations. It behooves the Christian to be conscientious and faithful in the discharge of all relative duties. And, as there is a necessity for intercourse and commerce among men, the virtues of justice and veracity should be constantly practiced, doing unto others as we would have them do unto us [Luke 6:31]. And, in social intercourse, to promote good fellowship, there should be real kindness, respectfulness, candor, and courtesy, assiduously cultivated. The standing rule should be to do nothing and say nothing which would tend to the injury of our neighbor, but continually to seek to promote his best interests.

Man is utterly unable to perform works of supererogation. When he has done all that is commanded, he must acknowledge himself to be an unprofitable servant, having done no more than it was his duty to do.

CHAPTER 27

Prayer

Prayer is a duty dictated by reason. If a child is hungry and wants bread, nature impels it to go to his or her parent for a supply; and the natural affections of parents to their offspring render them prompt to answer such requests. Even if they intended beforehand to give the necessary food, in proper season, it is nevertheless pleasing to them that the child should feel its dependence, and come and ask for what he or she needs. If this is seen by all to be reasonable and becoming in children toward earthly parents, how much more reasonable and becoming that we should feel our dependence for every good thing on our heavenly Father, and should go to Him and ask Him to grant us such things as are necessary for our present and eternal welfare. On this very principle does our Lord urge upon His disciples the duty of praying for the Holy Spirit, in which gift all spiritual blessings are comprehended. His words are, "And I say unto you, Ask, and it shall be given you; seek, and ye shall find; knock, and it shall be opened unto you. For every one that asketh receiveth; and he that seeketh findeth; and to him that knocketh it shall be opened. If a son shall ask bread of any of you that is a father, will he give him a stone? or if he ask a fish, will he for a fish give him a serpent? or if he shall ask an egg will he offer him a scorpion? If ye then, being evil, know how to give good gifts unto your children: how much more shall your heavenly Father give the Holy Spirit to them that ask him?" [Luke 11:9-13].

Prayer is no more inconsistent with the unchangeable purposes of God than the use of any other means; for God in forming His purposes had respect to all appropriate means of producing the intended ends, and among these, prayer has an important place.

It is a low idea of the efficacy of prayer to confine it to the good effect which it is adapted to produce on the feelings of the person who offers it. Indeed, if this were believed to be the whole benefit derived from prayer, a great part of the good impression which it makes on the petitioner would be lost. As we obtain the things which we need from earthly parents by asking; so also, we receive the blessings which we need from our heavenly Father by praying for them.

In how many instances did Moses, by his prayers, avert the judgments of God from the Israelites. The prophet Samuel also, by prayer, obtained a signal victory for the people of Israel over their enemies. But no single instance of the efficacy of prayer recorded in Scripture is more remarkable than that of the prophet Elijah. This case is referred to by the apostle James in the following manner: "The effectual fervent prayer of a righteous man availeth much. Elias was a man subject to like passions as we are, and he prayed earnestly that it might not rain: and it rained not on the earth by the space of three years and six months. And he prayed again, and the heaven gave rain, and the earth brought forth her fruit" [James 5:16-18].

In prayer may be properly comprehended all devotional acts of the mind, and the suitable expression of these sentiments in external gestures and words. Adoration is one of the most suitable and solemn feelings of which a creature is capable, when he comes into the presence of the august majesty of Heaven.

Godly fear, or reverence, is another feeling which must be experienced when any just idea is entertained of the almighty power, terrible majesty, and awe-inspiring holiness of the Creator. Penitent confession is so appropriate to sinners in their approaches to God, that no one can have any sense of the divine character and presence without falling down before Him, under a deep impression of entire unworthiness. Even the holiest men, such as Isaiah, Daniel, and the apostle John, were overwhelmed with a feeling of unworthiness when God manifested Himself to them with something of His majesty and glory.

Praise and thanksgiving are exercises of devotion which must be excited into lively exercise in every pious mind, by the consideration of the wonderful works and munificent dispensations of our heavenly Father; and especially our praise and thanksgiving are due for redeeming love. This part of our devotional exercises will be continued through eternity. The song begun here will rise to its noblest strains when the saints in heaven, redeemed by the blood of Christ and saved by His power, shall, in one grand chorus, sing, "Unto him that loved us, and washed us from our sins in his own blood, and hath made us kings and priests unto God and his Father, to him be glory and dominion for ever and ever. Amen" [Rev. 1:5-6].

But that which is more properly denominated prayer is petition. We approach the throne of grace to ask for such things as we need. Prayer has, therefore, been very correctly defined to be "the offering up of our desires unto God, in the name of Christ, for things agreeable to his will" [SC 98]. Desire itself is not prayer, but the expression of our desires to God, is the essence of prayer. In this there are several things to be considered.

When there is strong desire, there is a feeling of want. Man has nothing for which he is not dependent. He needs many things for the welfare and comfort of his body. These wants are supplied by the beneficent dispensations of divine providence. For these blessings he is permitted to ask: "Give us day by day our daily bread" [Luke 11:3]. As to the extent of earthly blessings, he should ask only for what is necessary, and may be for his own good, and the glory of God. When deprived of health or other temporal blessings, he may seek for deliverance and for a restoration of such favors as have been withheld; but as it is good to be afflicted, he should pray more to have his sufferings sanctified than removed.

Our prayers should be chiefly offered for spiritual blessings, for ourselves and others. Here we cannot be too importunate. We are taught, indeed, that it is importunity in prayer which secures the blessing. This includes earnestness and perseverance. We should pray and not faint; be instant in prayer; yea, pray without ceasing. Prayer, to the spiritual life, is like breathing to the life of the body. We cannot live without prayer. Our prayers should not be confined to ourselves and our immediate connections. These may properly hold a first place in our petitions; but we are bound to pray for rulers, and for all that are in authority, and for all sorts of men, that God would be merciful to them, and show them His salvation.

Prayer should be in the name of Christ. Faith is absolutely necessary in acceptable prayer, and faith always has respect to the Mediator. The humble penitent feels that he is unworthy to approach the throne of God in his own name, for he is defiled with sin. He can only come with liberty and confidence, when he beholds his great High Priest standing between him and the divine Majesty. The prayers of believers are rendered acceptable and efficacious only through the intercession of Jesus Christ, our advocate. This is the precious incense which is offered with the prayers of all saints.

But faith has respect also to the promises of God. On these it firmly relies, believing that what He hath said, He will faithfully perform. The person who prays in faith, confidently expects to receive whatever God has promised to give, in answer to prayer. Christians should therefore watch for the answer to their petitions. They should be attentive to the providences of God, by which prayer is often answered.

Prayer was never intended to supersede the use of other means; effort should always follow our prayers. The more faithfully we labor, the better reason have we to expect an answer to prayer.

CHAPTER 28

Assurance of Salvation

We read in the Epistle to the Hebrews, both of the "assurance of faith" [Heb. 10:22] and the "assurance of hope" [Heb. 6:11]. As faith is itself a belief of the truth, the assurance of faith can signify nothing else than a strong faith, an undoubting conviction of the truth. As hope is an expectation of future good, which may be more or less strong, as the evidence that the good hoped for shall be ours, the assurance of hope is a full persuasion that in due time we shall realize the blessing which we desire. According to this interpretation, the assurance of hope does not differ from the assurance of salvation.

The relation between the assurance of faith and the assurance of hope is hence manifest. The former is the necessary foundation of the latter. Unless we are fully persuaded that there is a full and suitable salvation in Christ, it is impossible that we should be assured that we shall obtain salvation through Him. But as God promises eternal life to every one who believes in Christ, when we do sincerely believe, and when our faith is strong, it is easy to draw the inference that the salvation of the gospel is ours. The thing stands thus. God says, "He that believeth...shall be saved" [Mark 16:16]. I am conscious that I believe; therefore, I know that I shall be saved. The strength of this conclusion, or the assurance that I shall obtain salvation, depends first on the assurance which I have that there is salvation in Christ for everyone that believes. If I receive this declaration with some degree of dubiety, then there being no assurance of faith, of course, there can be no assurance of salvation. But if this truth be received, without any wavering, then there is a solid foundation on which the assurance of hope may rest.

In the next place, having believed in the promise of God, I must know certainly that I have believed, and that my faith is genuine. For although I believe ever so certainly in the truth of God's promise of eternal life to him that believeth, yet, if I doubt whether I have believed, or am uncertain whether my faith is of that kind to which the promise is made, I cannot possess assurance of salvation. There seems to be some ground for a doubt of this kind, as we read of several kinds of faith which were not connected with salvation. One species of faith which was not saving, is represented as being accompanied with joy and every appearance of being genuine, until being put to the trial, it was found to be deficient.

Again, it ought to be remarked here, that many persons have entertained a strong persuasion that they were the heirs of salvation, and yet their confidence was founded in error or delusion. Therefore, although at first view, it would seem the easiest thing in the world for a true believer to arrive at assurance of salvation, yet when we take into view the deceitfulness of the heart, and the power of Satan to transform himself into an angel of light, and also the numerous cases of actual deception which have occurred, we are so far from thinking it easy to arrive at assurance, that we are disposed to believe that an infallible, unwavering assurance, on solid scriptural grounds, can be acquired by no one, without the special witness of the Holy Spirit. Most Christians, at least in our day, do not possess an assurance of salvation which excludes all doubt and fear as to their future destiny. They have attained to a comfortable hope, but not to the assurance of hope — except at some favored moments, when the love of God is shed abroad in their heart, by the Holy Ghost sent down from heaven. Then the Spirit witnesses with their spirits, that they are the children of God.

How this witness is given, is a matter concerning which there are different opinions. But as there are spurious joys which may be very ecstatic, it is safest to believe that this assurance is commonly given by bringing into lively exercise, faith, love, and joy; so that there can be no doubt of the existence of these exercises, as there can be none, that they are feelings peculiar to the children of God. The Spirit not only enlightens the mind to discern the beauty of holiness in the Word, but also to discern the image of the truth made on the heart, so that by His illumination, the believer is enabled to look back on his past experience, and to see, that, from time to time, he has exercised true faith, love, etc.; or, that he now actually is in the exercise of these graces. I do not, however, see any reason to doubt that God may sometimes, without any examination or comparison of its exercises with the marks of His Word, fill the soul of the believer with a joyful persuasion of His love, and may so pour into it the Spirit of adoption, that it shall be enabled, with filial confidence, to cry, "Abba, Father." Many testimonies to this purpose might be collected from the experience of saints.

But alas, many serious, conscientious persons are always more or less under a cloud of doubt and uncertainty respecting their spiritual condition. These broken reeds must not be crushed, nor this smoking flax quenched, by any doctrine of ours; for often among these are found the truly contrite and humble spirits with whom Jehovah delights to take up His abode. Where doubting does not arise from any want of confidence in the truth of God's Word, but altogether from diffidence of the genuineness of our own faith, it does not partake of the nature of unbelief; for there is so much reason to distrust our own hearts, that this timidity and uncertainty is often rather an evidence of self-knowledge and humility than of unbelief. Still, such persons are deprived of much comfort, which Christians ought to enjoy. These doubts are very distressing, and do not qualify the person to exhibit the bright side of religion to those around him. No person should be contented to remain under this dark cloud which so obscures his future prospects. Assurance of salvation is attainable by all true believers who assiduously seek it. Let all then strive to obtain this inestimable blessing.

The true doctrine of assurance is taught in the Westminster Larger Catechism, and is clearly expressed in the following words, "Such as truly believe in Christ, and endeavour to walk in all good conscience before Him, may, without extraordinary revelation, by faith grounded on the truth of God's promises, and by the Spirit enabling them to discern in themselves those graces to which the promises of life are made, and bearing witness with their spirits that they are the children of God, be infallibly assured that they are in a state of grace, and shall persevere therein unto salvation" [LC 80].

Again, "Assurance of grace and salvation, not being of the essence of faith, true believers may wait long before they obtain it; and after the enjoyment thereof, may have it weakened and intermitted through manifold distempers, sins, temptations and desertions; yet are they never left without such a presence and support of the Spirit of God, as keeps them from sinking into utter despair" [LC 81].

That assurance of salvation is attainable in this life is very evident from the Scriptures, both of the Old and New Testaments. Indeed, all the saints, of whom any expression of their spiritual state is recorded, appear to have possessed a full sense of their reconciliation and acceptance with God. The only doubt is whether they owed their assurance to that supernatural inspiration which they possessed, or to clear revelations to them personally, that they were the adopted and beloved children of God. We know that in some cases such communications were made to individual saints, as to Abel, Noah, Abraham, Isaiah, and Daniel; but the mere possession of miraculous gifts furnished no decisive evidence of the spiritual state of the persons who had received these gifts. We know that Balaam, who loved the wages of unrighteousness, prophesied by the inspiration of God; and Judas, the traitor, received the same commission as the other disciples to heal the sick, to cast out devils, and to raise the dead. Moreover, our Lord assures us that at the last day, some will make this a plea for admittance into His heavenly kingdom, that in His name they had cast out devils and done many wonderful works, but He will say unto them, "I never knew you: depart from me, ye that work iniquity" [Matt. 7:23].

Paul's strong assurance seems to have been the effect of that faith which he possessed in common with other Christians. He felt it to be necessary to work out his salvation with fear and trembling, and to keep his body under, lest after preaching to others, he himself should become a castaway [1 Cor. 9:27]. His assurance of a crown of life at the appearing of Christ was founded on the consciousness of having fought a good fight and having kept the faith. The faith of the apostles was of the same kind as that of Christians at the present time; the only difference was in its strength. As the apostles had nothing but what they had gratuitously received, there is no reason known to us why God may not grant as great grace to some persons in modern times as was bestowed on the primitive Christians, or even on the apostles.

From the view of assurance which has been given above, it may be inferred that the true reason why so many sincere Christians in our day live without assurance is the feebleness of their faith. They need, therefore, to be exhorted, in the language of the apostle Peter, "Wherefore the rather, brethren, give diligence to make your calling and election sure" [2 Pet. 1:10].

The apostle John teaches us how we may obtain this precious grace of assurance. "We know that we have passed from death unto life, because we love the brethren" [1 John 3:14]. "If our heart condemn us not, then have we confidence toward God" [1 John 3:21]. "My little children, let us not love in word, neither in tongue; but in deed and in truth. And hereby we know that we are of the truth, and shall assure our hearts before him" [1 John 3:18-19].

Some exercised Christians fail to obtain assurance by mistaking the evidences of true piety; or rather, by supposing that the working of inward corruption, of which they are conscious, is inconsistent with a state of grace. A correct knowledge of the marks and evidences of true religion is of great importance to obtain a settled assurance.

Some humble Christians possess this blessing without giving it its proper name. The writer recollects a conversation which passed in his presence between an eminent minister of the gospel and an old lady who had been converted under the ministry of the Rev. Samuel Davies. This old lady had given indubitable evidence of eminent piety for more than half a century but she said to the clergyman who was conversing with her, "I have never attained to the faith of assurance— mine is only the faith of reliance." To which the clergyman answered, "If you know you have the faith of reliance, you have the faith of assurance."

Some persons seem to expect assurance in some extraordinary way by an immediate divine revelation, or by a voice from heaven. But this is enthusiasm. John Flavel makes mention of a young man who most earnestly sought for some extraordinary evidence of his acceptance with God; as he walked in the fields he vainly hoped that the very stones would speak, so that he might know whether he was a child of God. But afterwards, convinced of his error, he sought this blessing in the way of self-examination, reading the Scriptures and using other appointed means, and was not disappointed; for in the use of instituted means he attained to a settled and comfortable assurance of his interest in Christ.

It may be remarked here that assurance is not always accompanied with joy. There may be a scriptural conviction that a work of divine grace has been experienced, and at the same moment there may be no strong affections, nor any very vigorous actings of faith. This may be called habitual assurance. But there is in the experience of many, at times, a joyful persuasion of the mercy and favor of God. This is probably what is meant by having "the love of God shed abroad in our hearts by the Holy Ghost which is given unto us" [Rom. 5:5]. Such seasons are very precious, but never last long.

It is a sad case when assurance is enjoyed for a while, and then is lost through sin or carelessness. This is often experienced by backsliders. Assurance can never be enjoyed by those who depart from God, even though the root of the matter be in them. When a comfortable sense of the divine favor is lost, it is hard to recover it. Such Christians often walk mournfully, with their heads bowed down as a bulrush, to the close of life. After his woeful lapse, David cried, "Cast me not away from thy presence; and take not thy holy spirit from me. Restore unto me the joy of thy salvation; and uphold me with thy free spirit" [Ps. 51:11-12]. "Make me to hear joy and gladness; that the bones which thou hast broken may rejoice" [Ps. 51:8].

Many pious souls, there is reason to believe, are depressed and their evidences beclouded by a melancholy temperament. Physical causes necessarily have a powerful effect on the exercises of the mind; this is felt in religion, as well as in other things.

CHAPTER 29

Perseverance of the Saints

This subject is intimately connected with the assurance of salvation. For if true believers may lose their faith and totally and finally fall away, then, manifestly, there can be no such thing as assurance of salvation. Some say that a person may know assuredly that he is a child of God and at present free from all condemnation, but upon this hypothesis, he cannot possibly be assured that he will continue in this happy state. In the exercise of his own free will, he may depart from God, renounce Christ, and become a reprobate. If this doctrine be admitted that all saints are liable to apostatize, and that there is no such thing promised as the grace of perseverance, then Paul's declarations, in which he expresses the fullest confidence that he should possess a crown of life, must be understood conditionally: provided he should persevere to the end. In the same manner we must construe those triumphant expressions of Romans 8:38-39, "For I am persuaded, that neither death, nor life, nor angels, nor principalities, nor powers, nor things present, nor things to come, nor height, nor depth, nor any other creature, shall be able to separate us from the love of God, which is in Christ Jesus our Lord." According to this theory, we must understand the apostle to mean that if he continued in the faith, none of these things should be able to separate him from the love of God in Christ Jesus. But who knows whether Paul did persevere to the end? Who knows but that his faith failed in the last extremity? We have no account in the New Testament of the circumstances of his death. Indeed, if the standing of believers depends on themselves, it would not be surprising that any one should be overcome by temptation and should finally fall from a state of grace. It is possible, then, that all the apostles might have fallen away in the time of persecution; for although Christ promises to go and prepare a place for them, and that they should sit on thrones in His kingdom, yet all this must be understood on condition they persevered to the end!

Those who maintain that all true believers will certainly persevere, do not ground their opinion on any ability which any of them have to stand. Left to themselves, they believe, all of them would be sure to apostatize.

They attribute perseverance in grace, as they do the first conversion of the soul, to the love of God. They believe that the same power which brings the soul from death to life is able to preserve it in life; and that the gifts and callings of God are without repentance, that is, without change of purpose [Rom. 11:29].

Again, as believers are intimately and spiritually united to Christ, so as to be members of His mystical body, and since in virtue of this union they receive continual supplies of grace and strength as they need these blessings, they are of the opinion, that Christ the Head will never suffer any member actually united to Him, to be severed from His body and to perish forever.

Surely the Spirit of all grace which dwells in believers is sufficient to keep up that spiritual life which He has generated in them, and is able to keep them from the danger of apostasy. If He can do this, He will do it; for whom He loves, He loves to the end.

Those whose names are written in heaven in the Lamb's Book of Life, before the foundation of the world, will at last reach heaven. The kingdom, which the saints shall inherit, was prepared for them before the foundation of the world.

Not one link of Paul's glorious chain of salvation can be broken. "Whom he did foreknow, he also did predestinate to be conformed to the image of his Son.... Moreover whom he did predestinate, them he also called: and whom he called, them he also justified: and whom he justified, them he also glorified" [Rom. 8:29-30].

The apostle Paul was confident that He who had begun a good work in the Philippians would perform it until the day of Jesus Christ. Can it be believed, that the same love and power which effectually called believers from their death in sin, will not preserve them in a state of spiritual life when it has been commenced?

In the days of the apostles there were many apostates; but John, in 1 John 2:19, clearly teaches that such had never been sincere Christians: "They went out from us, but they were not of us; for if they had been of us, they would no doubt have continued with us; but they went out, that they might be made manifest that they were not all of us." And the apostle Paul, in 2 Timothy 2:19, treating of the success of heretics in subverting the faith of some, that is, seducing them to embrace false doctrines, will by no means agree that these persons who were thus led astray, or their teachers, had ever belonged to the foundation of God, or were among His approved people; for he says, "Nevertheless, the foundation of God standeth sure, having this seal, The Lord knoweth them that are his" [2 Tim 2:19].

But it is said by the impugners of this doctrine that though God will not forsake His people, yet they may forsake Him; that the promises are made to the people of God, but when they cease to be His people, they cut themselves off from the blessings of the covenant of grace, which are all conditional, and made to *believers*. Now, we admit that if any should cease to believe, they would be thus cut off; but we maintain that their faith shall never fail. If God has made promises to this effect, then they are safe. We know that Christ by His intercession did keep Peter's faith from utterly failing, for He said, "I have prayed for thee, that thy faith fail not" [Luke 22:32]. And His intercessions were not only for Peter and the apostles, but for all who should through their word believe on His name. And in Jeremiah 32:40, we find an explicit promise and solemn covenant in which God engages to preserve His people from falling: "And I will make an everlasting covenant with them, that I will not turn away from them, to do them good." This seems to be a very full promise and a covenant in all things well-ordered and sure. But this is not all; He immediately adds, "but I will put my fear in their hearts, *that they shall not depart from me*." And this seems to be implied, when He promised, "I will put my laws in their mind, and write them in their hearts" [Heb. 8:10].

In John 10, our blessed Lord speaks of Himself as the good Shepherd. He gives as the chief characteristic of a good shepherd that he loves his sheep. In His own case, His love was so great that He was willing to lay down His life for the sheep. Furthermore, He informs us that those who were truly of the number of His sheep would hear His voice and follow Him, while they would not hear the voice of strangers. His attention to the flock as their Shepherd was so kind and compassionate that He calls each one by his name and goes before the sheep, and leads them in the right way. From this description, it can be inferred that Christ would not forsake those on whom He had set His love and that He would not suffer their enemies to carry them off. Those persons who were specially the purchase of His blood and His dying agonies, He would certainly be disposed to save from perdition. There can be no doubt the desire of the great Shepherd is that these objects of His love, for whom He had paid a price above all estimation, should not perish.

But we are not left to our own inferences on this subject. Our blessed Lord has anticipated our conclusions by His clear and positive declarations. His gracious words should never be forgotten: "My sheep hear my voice, and I know them, and they follow me: and I give unto them eternal life; *and they shall never perish*, neither shall any man pluck them out of my hand. My Father, which gave them me, is greater than all; and no man is able to pluck them out of my Father's hand" [John 10:27-29]. I do not know how the doctrine of the saints' perseverance could be expressed in stronger language. It must be evident that if God is able to keep them from perishing, they will be saved. And who will dare to call in question the ability of Christ and His Father to preserve whom He will from apostatizing?

170 A Brief Compendium of Bible Truth

Surely God is able to cause even the weakest of them to stand.

Suppose the contrary; suppose that one of these given by the Father to His only begotten Son to be redeemed, should be overcome by Satan, the enemy of God and His people, and should perish eternally. What a triumph to the grand adversary, and what a dishonor to the Redeemer! Shall it ever be said in the world of woe, "Here is one of the beloved of God, specially given to the Son, purchased with the blood of the Son of God, raised from the death of sin by the power of His Spirit —yes, one who heard His voice, loved and followed Him, who is eternally lost! The Savior was not able to preserve this soul from falling under the power of temptation. In this contest, Satan gained the victory and tore away one of Christ's beloved sheep—yes, dismembered His mystical body; for this soul, now damned, was once a member of the body of Christ"? Reader, can you believe this? Do not these arguments convince you that such a thing as this never can occur?

Again, does not Christ appear in heaven as the Advocate of His people? Does not the Father hear Him always? And shall not His intercessions be effectual to obtain persevering grace for all those whose cause He pleads? "He is able also to save them to the uttermost that come unto God by him, seeing he ever liveth to make intercession for them" [Heb. 7:25]. It is the continual intercession of Christ that preserves His disciples from falling away totally and finally. Peter in his self-confidence fell into an enormous and disgraceful sin; and if he had been left to himself, Satan would undoubtedly have overcome him and ruined him.

That Christ intercedes for believers as He does not for others, we learn from that remarkable intercessory prayer which He offered before He left the world: "I pray for them: I pray not for the world, but for them which thou hast given me; for they are thine. And all mine are thine, and thine are mine; and I am glorified in them. While I was with them in the world, I kept them in thy name: those that thou gavest me I have kept, and none of them is lost, but the son of perdition" [John 17:9-10, 12]. Those who oppose the doctrine which we now defend, think that in this last clause the nerves of the argument drawn from this passage are cut; and that as Judas was one of those given to Christ by His Father, and he perished, therefore believers may eternally perish. But can any impartial, intelligent Christian believe that Judas was really included in the number of those given to Christ by the Father, and for whom He prayed? This construction would not only be dishonorable to Christ, but it would destroy the force and consistency of all that Christ uttered in this remarkable prayer. If Christ prayed not for the world, how came He to pray for Judas, who was a thief and covetous from the time of his being first called to be an apostle? Christ had perfect knowledge of his hypocrisy. And if He specially prayed for him, as much as for the other disciples, how did it come to pass that this prayer was ineffectual in his case?

If Christ's special intercessions may be ineffectual, what solid ground do we have to trust in Him, and why was it declared that the Father hears Him always? But it will be asked, how do we get over the difficulty which this clause presents? If the original Greek be construed agreeably to the common usage of the language, there will remain no difficulty. The sentence is elliptical, and the true import undoubtedly is, "And none of them is lost: but the son of perdition is lost, who was not of the number given." The very same construction is used, where our Lord says, "Many widows were in Israel in the days of Elias...but unto none of them was Elias sent, save unto Sarepta, a city of Sidon, unto a woman that was a widow" [Luke 4:25-26]. The *save* here excludes the widow of Sarepta, for she was not a widow of Israel, but belonged to the Canaanitish nation. And in the same context we read, "And many lepers were in Israel in the time of Eliseus the prophet; and none of them was cleansed, saving Naaman the Syrian" (Luke 4:27). Naaman was not one of the lepers of Israel, but a man of a foreign nation, just as Judas was not one whom the Savior had kept, but was the son of perdition. This text, therefore, properly understood, furnishes no objection whatever to the doctrine of the saints' perseverance derived from this intercessory prayer of our Lord. This prayer itself affords an impregnable foundation for this precious doctrine.

It is hard to believe that those whose names were written in the Lamb's book of life before the foundation of the world shall utterly and eternally perish. It is promised to the saints of the church of Sardis that their names shall not be blotted out of the book of life, and it is reasonable to think that the same promise is applicable to all true believers. If these names might be blotted out, there would be no great cause of rejoicing that they were written in heaven, but our Lord teaches His disciples to rejoice in this, above all things (Luke 10:20).

Revelation 22:19 says, "And if any man shall take

away from the words of the book of this prophecy, God shall take away his part out of the book of life, and out of the holy city, and from the things which are written in this book." The meaning is not that such a person ever had any part in this book, but that he never should have. It is not said that the names of such were written in the book of life, but it is declared that it was a privilege of which they should never partake.

There is one view of this subject which I have not seen given by the authors I have consulted. When created, all accountable creatures are placed in a state of probation. When this probation is ended, they are confirmed in a state of holiness and happiness, and are never again exposed to any peril with regard to their eternal life. Thus, when a part of the angels fell, the remaining hosts were confirmed, and are therefore called "elect angels" [1 Tim. 5:21]. Whether they stood by their own inherent strength, or whether some gratuitous aid was afforded to them which was not granted to those who fell, as some suppose, we cannot certainly tell. But all seem to be agreed that the holy angels are no longer exposed to any danger of perishing.

In the case of mankind, if our federal head and representative had retained his innocence and finished his obedience, even to the end of the time appointed for his trial, it seems to be agreed by most that there would have been no trial of each individual. All the human race would have been brought into existence in a justified state—not only in a state of innocence, but in a state of confirmed holiness, liable to no danger of sinning or perishing. Now since the second Adam, the Representative and Surety of His chosen seed, has rendered a complete righteousness to the law, when the same is imputed to His people for their justification, will they not stand at least in as safe a condition as they would have been in had their first representative fulfilled the condition of the covenant of works? It appears reasonable to think that no justified persons ever can fall away, for God is engaged to grant them eternal life, and has covenanted to prevent them, by His confirming grace, from falling into sin and ruin.

Before he sinned, Adam was not in a justified state, though in a state of innocence, because his probation was not yet ended. So also we suppose that the fallen angels were never in a justified state; they also fell before their probation was finished. We know of no instance of a justified person ever perishing. And as believers are perfectly justified in Christ, they are no longer on probation for life; that is finished, and, therefore, they are included in the bonds of a covenant so well ordered, and so sure, that they can never perish.

Again, the sins of penitent believers are fully and absolutely pardoned; it is promised that these sins shall be forever buried and blotted out. But suppose one of these pardoned sinners to fall away from a state of grace: what will be his condition, in regard to the innumerable transgressions already pardoned? Will the guilt of these be laid upon the apostate, or not?

They who maintain the doctrine that true believers may finally fall away and perish, hold that God does all He consistently can to preserve them from apostatizing, and sincerely desires to bring them to the possession of eternal life. Now, I would ask, how is this consistent with acknowledged facts? Some Christians, while in the world, are exposed to much greater temptations than others. As God foreknew that certain persons would be unable to resist certain temptations by which they are supposed to be overcome, and caused finally to perish, why were they not preserved from such exposure by divine providence? But this is not all; some Christians are called away by death soon after their conversion and salvation are secured; others are left to be buffeted or seduced by temptations for many years, by which they are finally overcome, and are lost. Now if these had been taken out of the world at as early a period of their Christian pilgrimage as the former, they would also have been saved. Where is the impartiality of which so much is said, in relation to these?

This doctrine has been opposed on the principle that the belief of it tends to breed presumption and to encourage negligence in working out our salvation.

We do not assert that this doctrine has never been abused by unholy men; but what doctrine may not be thus abused? Certainly none more so than the love and mercy of God. In answer to this objection, we would observe that our doctrine is the perseverance of the saints in *faith* and *holiness*. Just so far as any professor fails in the exercise of faith and practice of holiness, he loses the evidence that he is a true Christian. According to this view of the subject, he never can persuade himself that he will persevere, unless he is in the exercise of grace, without which he cannot possess the evidences of being a true believer. Again, fear is not the only, nor the most efficacious motive which urges the Christian to activity and energy in running the gospel race. Hope has more influence on him than fear; and when his hope of final success arises to assurance, he is animated with the liveliest zeal, and impelled by the strongest motives, to lay aside every weight, and run with patience the race set before him.

This is consonant with experience in temporal matters. Suppose a man to have in prospect a journey through a very difficult and dangerous country. If he could be assured before setting out that however many obstacles and enemies he should encounter, he would certainly reach the end of his journey triumphantly, how would such assurance encourage his heart and nerve his body to go on courageously! Whereas, if he entertained but small hope of success, discouragement would weaken all his efforts.

It is acknowledged there are some texts of Scripture which, when viewed separately, seem to teach that true believers may fall from a state of grace; but the doctrine is so contrary to the great principles of the covenant of grace, that such an interpretation of any text as would favor it, cannot be admitted consistently with the analogy of divine truth. We must compare Scripture with Scripture, and thus endeavor to ascertain the mind of the Spirit. The apparent testimony of some texts of Scripture in favor of the apostasy of believers, led Augustine to adopt the opinion that some persons who are not of the number of the elect were really converted. Such people, however, never persevered to the end, but fell from the gracious state to which they had attained. He firmly maintained, however, that none of the elect could perish. Probably this opinion was adopted by Luther and some of his followers. Several have believed, that though the saints might for a season fall totally away, which they suppose must have been the case with David, Solomon, and Peter, yet they are always recovered, and never finally apostatize.

It is not necessary to make any remarks on this opinion, as it has been held by few. There are no instances in Scripture of the final fall of real saints. To such professors as will be found at the left hand of the Judge at the last day, it will be said, however great their gifts or privileges, "*I never knew you:* depart from me, ye that work iniquity " [Matt. 7:23]. How could this be said, if some of them had once been in union with Christ?

The texts of Scripture which seem to favor the final apostasy of real Christians, we have neither time nor space to consider in detail. We think, however, that they may all be explained in consistency with the true doctrine, upon one or more of the following principles. First, that the persons spoken of as righteous, or as believers, are described according to the opinion which they entertained of themselves, and the profession which they made. Second, that the cases are hypothetical, not declaring that any should actually fall away; but stating what would be the consequence if such an event should take place. Third, that the cases described are of those who, under the external light of divine revelation and the common influences of the Holy Spirit, had advanced far in the doctrinal knowledge of Christianity and had experienced lively impressions from the truth, without having undergone a radical change of heart. Such a case is described by our Savior in the parable of the sower, regarding those represented by the seed which fell on stony ground. They are those who hear the word with joy, and for a season, give pleasing evidence of piety, but having *no root in themselves*, fall away in the time of temptation.

To the above cases, we may add that of those, who in apostolic times, received the miraculous gifts of the

Holy Ghost; for these were not conferred only on real Christians, as we know from the case of Judas, and from the account given by our Lord of the plea which will be made by some whom he will condemn at the last day. They are represented as saying, "Have we not...in thy name...cast out devils? and in thy name done many wonderful works?" [Matt. 7:22]. Combine these two last cases and you have a satisfactory explanation of the character of those described in Hebrews 6. In all ages of the church, there are persons who greatly resemble true saints, not only in outward profession, but who have feelings and exercises which are well-devised counterfeits of the genuine piety of the heart.

But surely it never can be that one of those who were chosen in Christ, before the foundation of the world, called effectually in time and united to Christ so as to become living members of His mystical body; and whose sins He bore on the cross, and to whom He has promised the constant indwelling of the Holy Spirit, and whose names are in the book of life, should be finally lost. The enemy of God and man shall never, in the dark dominions over which he reigns, have it in his power to boast triumphantly that he has plucked from the hands of the great Shepherd one of the dear lambs of His flock. No, the elect of God cannot be deceived to their ruin. Those whose names are in the book of life shall never be cast into outer darkness. *"They shall never perish"* [John 10:28].

CHAPTER 30

The Sacraments

Sacraments are visible signs of invisible grace. They are also seals of God's covenant with men. Just as in more solemn transactions among men, besides the words in which the substance of the compact, or treaty, or deed of conveyance is contained, so it has been customary from the earliest times to have certain signs superadded to give solemnity to the transaction, and to deepen the impression of the obligations or stipulations into which the parties had entered. Frequently, such actions were performed as symbolically represented the consequences which would ensue from a violation of the contract, or a neglect of the duty promised. Thus, it was customary, not only in treaties between nations, but in the more important transactions among individuals, to have seals appended to bonds and contracts. Hence the joining of right hands and other ceremonies in marriage, and of wearing ribands or stars as a sign of some military order. We learn from Scripture that it was an ancient custom in forming solemn covenants to divide slaughtered animals and to cause the parties to pass between the dissected parts, by which it would seem an imprecation was implied that if either of the contracting parties should prove unfaithful, he would be cut to pieces in like manner. In accommodation to the nature and customs of men, God has, under every dispensation, appointed certain external rites which have no signification but in connection with the covenant to which they are appended. For these signs or symbolical actions are never found but in connection with solemn covenants which they are intended to confirm, or to render the ratification more solemn and impressive.

Another frequent use of institutions of this kind is to serve as memorials of events and transactions, which it was important should not be forgotten. We have many such in the Old Testament.

But as there is a resemblance readily conceived between certain objects or actions and certain truths, which is the foundation of figurative language, so this resemblance is the principle on which particular signs are adopted. Everybody, even a child, can see that washing the body, or a part of it, with pure water fitly represents the moral purification of the soul. As truth is gradually received, while some important things are future, it has pleased God to furnish a kind of faint prefiguration of such events which would serve to give some vague idea of the matter. Thus, by the presentment of an animal of a certain species before the altar, and then by the offerer confessing his sins over its head before it was slain, and by the sprinkling of blood by the priest, the vicarious atonement for sin was prefigured for ages before the real efficacious sacrifice was offered. By this ceremony being kept up daily before the eyes of the people, they were taught typically to look for redemption by the shedding of blood and to obtain pardon by having their sins transferred to another who would bear them away. Under the new dispensation there was less occasion for these ritual services; and, therefore, while the old ceremonial law was abolished, no new sacraments were instituted, except baptism and the Lord's Supper.

According to the universal testimony of Jewish writers, baptism was practiced by the Jews on the admission of proselytes, long before the advent of Jesus Christ. And, though circumcision was restricted to males, the ceremony of baptism was extended also to females, and, like circumcision, was administered to infants.

When John, the harbinger of the Messiah, was sent of God, he commenced his ministry by preaching repentance and baptism for the remission of sins. The object of his mission was "to prepare the way of the Lord" [Matt. 3:3; Mark 1:3; Luke 3:4] by arousing the attention of the people, and bringing about a reformation in the nation. His baptism was a national baptism. It was the duty of all the people to repent and submit to this rite, which they generally did. The Pharisees and lawyers, however, rejected the counsel of God, not being baptized of John.

Commanded by Christ's own direction, the disciples administered baptism to such as acknowledged Christ to be the Messiah. But baptism, as a rite of the Christian church, did not exist until the new dispensation commenced, which was not until after Christ's resurrection. Then a new commission was given to the apostles, "Go ye therefore, and teach all nations, baptizing them in the name of the Father, and of the Son, and of the Holy Ghost" [Matt. 28:19]. This was properly the institution of Christian baptism, and differed from the rite as formerly administered in two respects: first, in being in the name of the adorable Trinity, and, secondly, in being made a badge of discipleship in the

Christian church, or a formal initiation into the visible church of Christ. The Westminster Larger Catechism says, "Baptism is not to be administered to any that are out of the visible church until they profess their faith in Christ and obedience to him; but the children of such as are members of the visible church are to be baptized" [LC 166].

CHAPTER 31

Baptism

There has always been a tendency to make too much of these external rites and to depend unduly upon them, as a ground on which to hope for salvation. Thus, the Jews so exalted the importance of the rite of circumcision that they seem to have thought that being descended from Abraham and having this sign in their flesh insured their salvation. Christ and His apostles labored to overthrow this confidence. It is no wonder, therefore, that the same error should arise in regard to baptism. In the New Testament, baptism is both a duty and a privilege, but no undue importance is given to it, nor any undue efficacy ascribed to it. Paul spent little of his time in administering this rite. He avoided it at Corinth, where there were divisions and factions, lest any should say that he baptized in his own name. And he says expressly that Christ sent him "not to baptize, but to preach the gospel" [1 Cor. 1:17], which single declaration is a refutation of the opinion that internal grace, or regeneration, always accompanies baptism; for in that case, baptism would be far more important than preaching. Paul certainly could not convey grace by preaching; but if he could have regenerated all to whom he administered baptism, he should have given himself up entirely to this work. These sacramental institutions are not intended to be the means of conveying grace to the subjects in some mysterious manner, but they are intended to operate on adults by the Word of truth, which accompanies the ordinance.

Some lay a great stress on the mode in which baptism is administered, insisting that a total immersion of the body in water is essential to the right administration. In the ceremonies of a sacrament, some things belong to its essence because they represent symbolically the truth intended to be impressed on the mind; other things are indifferent, because they are merely incidental and do not affect the import of the sacrament. If it could be proved that the act of immersion was the thing in the ceremony which is principally significant of the truth intended to be inculcated, it would be essential. But if the mode of applying water has nothing to do with the emblematical signification of the ordinance, it is an indifferent circumstance; as much so as whether baptism be administered in a vessel or in a river; or whether in the Lord's Supper, leavened or unleavened bread be used; or whether we recline or sit upright in partaking of this ordinance. With regard to indifferent, incidental circumstances which do not enter into the essence of the sacrament, there is no obligation to follow what all know was the practice of Christ and the apostles; as it is certain that in the first institution of the sacred supper, they reclined on couches, used unleavened bread, and partook of it in the evening. We do not feel bound to imitate any of these things.

The baptism of the children of those who themselves were in covenant with God, though not expressly mentioned in Scripture, is a practice supported by good and sufficient reasons. It cannot be supposed that under the gospel dispensation, the privileges of the offspring of believers are less than under the Jewish. But we know that by God's command, circumcision, the sign of the covenant, was administered to all the males. They were thus brought externally within the bonds of the covenant; and although the external rite of initiation has been changed, there is no intimation given that the children of believers were to be henceforth excluded from the visible church.

Christ was displeased with His disciples for hindering little children to come unto him, "for," said He, "of such is the kingdom of God. And he took them up in his arms, put his hands upon them, and blessed them" [Mark 10:14, 16].

Household baptism was practiced by the apostles, and children form a part of most households.

Infants are depraved and need the washing of regeneration, and are capable of being regenerated; and this renovation, baptism does strikingly represent. The practice may be traced back to the earliest period of the church, and was then universal in all parts of the world. It is scarcely credible that so great a change should have become universal in the church, without being noticed by writers of ecclesiastical history.

CHAPTER 32

The Lord's Supper

When Christ celebrated the passover for the last time with His disciples, at the close of the feast, He instituted another sacrament, bearing a strong analogy to this Jewish festival, to be perpetually observed in His church until He should come again. While they were reclining around the table, He took of the bread which remained, blessed and brake it, and gave it to His disciples, saying, "This is my body which is given for you: this do in remembrance of me. Likewise also the cup after supper, saying, This cup is the new testament in my blood, which is shed for you" [Luke 22:19, 20]. As this ordinance was intended to be social, that is, to be celebrated by the church when assembled, Paul calls it a communion: "The cup of blessing which we bless, is it not the communion of the blood of Christ? The bread which we break, is it not the communion of the body of Christ?" [1 Cor. 10:16].

Nothing can be plainer than the nature of the duty enjoined upon the disciples, and intended to be obligatory on all Christians to the end of the world; for the apostle Paul, who was not present at the institution of the eucharist, but received it, as he did the gospel, by immediate revelation, when he recites the words of institution, adds an important clause, "For as often as ye eat this bread, and drink this cup, ye do shew the

Lord's death till he come" [1 Cor. 11:26]. From these words it is evident that Holy Communion was intended to be a standing memorial of the death of Christ until His second advent.

When Christ says, "This is my body" [Matt. 26:26; Mark 14:22; Luke 22:19; 1 Cor. 11:24] to suppose that He meant to teach that the piece of bread which He held in His hand was literally His material body, is an opinion so monstrous and involving so many contradictions, that it never could have originated but in a dark and superstitious age. In the first place, it was contradicted by all the senses, for the properties of bread and wine remained after the words were spoken, just the same as before. In all other cases of miracles, the appeal is to the senses: no example can be adduced of men being required to believe anything contrary to the testimony of their senses. But if the bread which Christ held in His hand was literally His body, He must have had two bodies; for if He partook of the bread, He must have eaten His own body. He says, "This is my body, which is broken for you" [1 Cor. 11:24]. "This is my blood of the new testament, which is shed for many" [Mark 14:24]. If these words are taken literally, then Christ was already slain, and His blood already shed; He was, therefore, crucified before He was nailed to the cross. Moreover, if the bread is transubstantiated every time this sacrament is celebrated, Christ must have as many bodies as there are officiating priests; and while His body is glorified in heaven, it is offered as a sacrifice on earth, in thousands of different places. While Christ's glorified body in heaven is no longer composed of flesh and blood, the body made out of the bread and wine, is a real body of flesh containing blood, as when

He tabernacled among men. And if the thing were possible, what spiritual benefit could be derived from devouring flesh? From its nature, being material, it could not nourish the spiritual life. And when received into the stomach as food, what becomes of it? Is it incorporated, like common food, into our bodies? I will not pursue the subject further. Before a man can believe in transubstantiation, he must abandon his reason and his senses.

Withholding the cup from the laity is an open violation of our Lord's command and a manifest mutilation of the ordinance. The pretense for this presumptuous departure from the express command of Christ is both superstitious and impious, for it implies that in the institution of the cup Christ was lacking in wisdom, or that He underestimated the danger of having His blood desecrated by being spilt.

As the Lord's Supper is a memorial of the death of Christ, it should be celebrated often, so that this great sacrifice on which our salvation depends may not be forgotten, but kept in lively remembrance in the Christian church.

If it be inquired in what sense Christ is present in the eucharist, we answer, spiritually, to those who by faith apprehend and receive Him. The idea of a bodily presence in, with, or under the bread and wine, is little less absurd than the doctrine of transubstantiation. Indeed, in some respects, it is even more impossible, for it requires and supposes the ubiquity of Christ's body. The truth therefore, is that only they who exercise faith in Christ, as exhibited in the eucharist, eat His flesh and drink His blood. A participation of the instituted signs, without faith to discern the Lord's body, is so far from being beneficial, that it involves the guilt of an awful crime; for "he that eateth and drinketh unworthily, eateth and drinketh damnation unto himself" [1 Cor. 11:29]. He is guilty of the body and blood of the Lord. "Let a man examine himself, and so let him eat of that bread, and drink of that cup" [1 Cor. 11:28].

To make a matter of importance of mere indifferent circumstances in the celebration of the sacraments has been the cause of useless and hurtful contentions. To insist on anything as necessary to a sacrament, which Christ has not expressly enjoined, is a wicked usurpation of His authority, by adding human inventions to divine ordinances.

The value of the Lord's Supper is incalculable. It is admirably adapted to our nature. It is simple, its meaning easily apprehended by the weakest minds. It is strongly significant and impressive. It has been called an epitome of the whole gospel, as the central truths of the system, in which all the rest are implied, are here clearly exhibited. And it ever has been signally blessed to the spiritual edification and comfort of the children of God. They, therefore, who neglect this ordinance, do at the same time disobey a positive command of Christ and deprive themselves of one of the richest privileges which can be enjoyed on this side of heaven.

CHAPTER 33

The Lord's Day and Divine Worship

Reason teaches that there is a God and that He ought to be worshipped. Had man remained in his primeval state of integrity, social worship would have been an incumbent duty. But from a survey of the constitution of man, it is evident that continual worship, whatever may be the fact in heaven, would not have been required of him while on the earth. The book of nature was spread out before him; and it would have been his duty to read daily those lessons which were taught by the heavens and the earth, the animal, vegetable, and mineral worlds. We know from express revelation that it was appointed to him to keep the garden of Eden, and dress it; and this would have required much attention, and vigorous exertion. It was never intended that man should lead an idle or inactive life. In the state of innocency, employment was as necessary to his happiness as it is now to the human race. He was also constituted lord of the inferior animals; the exercise of this dominion would of necessity occupy a portion of his time and attention. From a deliberate consideration of the circumstances in which man was placed, it may be legitimately inferred that in order to perform the primary duty of worshipping his Creator in that manner which was becoming and proper, he must have had some portion of his time appropriated to that service.

The worship due to the great Creator requires time for the contemplation of His attributes, as revealed in His glorious works. It requires time, also, to recollect all the manifestations of His wisdom and goodness in the dispensations of His providence, and to give vocal expression to feelings of gratitude for the benefits received and the happiness bestowed. No doubt, devotional feelings were habitual in the hearts of our first parents. No doubt, they sent up, more formally, their morning and evening prayers; but more time is needed to draw off the thoughts from visible things, and to concentrate them on the great invisible First Cause— the Giver of existence, and of all its capacities and enjoyments. Short snatches of time are not sufficient to perform this noblest of all duties in a proper manner. A whole day, at certain periods, was needed, so that there might be time for the contemplation of divine things, and for the full and free exercises of devotion. As man is a social being, and so constituted that by uniting with others who have the same views and feelings, his own through sympathy are rendered more animating and pleasing, it is evident that it was intended that mankind should worship and praise God in a general and public, as well as in an individual and private capacity. Now, it is too obvious to need proof that social worship requires stated times, known to all the people, when they may assemble for this divine employment. What proportion of time should be consecrated to this service, the reason of man, prior to experience, could not have determined. If it had been left free by the law of God, it would have been difficult to agree on the proportion; and if agreed upon, the obligation to set apart the due proportion of time would not have been so binding and sacred, as if the Almighty Creator should designate the day which should be employed in His service. Behold the amazing condescension of God! With some view to this very thing, He was pleased to perform the work of creation in six days, and to rest on the seventh; thus setting an example to His creature, man. He not only rested on the seventh day, but *sanctified* it; that is, set it apart to a holy use—to be employed, not in bodily labor or converse with the world, but in the contemplation of the works and attributes of God, and in holding delightful communion with his Maker. God could have commanded the world into existence with all its various furniture and species of living creatures in a single moment; but for man's sake, He created the heavens, the earth, the sea, the light, the air, vegetables, and animals in six successive days, and then ceased to work. Not that the Almighty could be weary or need rest; but for the purpose of teaching man that while he might lawfully spend six days in worldly employments, he must rest on the seventh day. This day, from the beginning, was a holy day. As the worship of God is the highest duty of man, the first express indication of the divine will in relation to man was that the seventh part of his time should be sacred to the service of his Creator.

The sabbath thus instituted as the very first provision for man's religious services, was the seventh from the commencement of the work of creation; but as man was made on the sixth day, the sabbath was his first day, after he saw light and breathed the air of heaven. This deserves particular notice, for it may have a connection with the change of the day of rest after the resurrection of Christ. The supposition is—and it is not given as a clearly revealed truth—that the first day of the week, according to human computation, was the day of rest from Adam to Moses; but that then, for some special reason, the day was changed to the seventh. Afterwards, when the Mosaic economy was terminated, at the resurrection of Christ, the original day, appointed at first to be the sabbath, was restored as a matter of course. Let every one exercise his own judgment on this point: it is no article of faith; but merely a probable conjecture.

It is surprising to find learned commentators trying to prove that no day was sanctified at the beginning; but that Moses mentions it in his history of the creation, by way of *prolepsis*, or anticipation. But this is an unnatural and forced construction, and invented without any cogent reason; for what absurd consequence follows the obvious meaning of the text? No, the absurdity, as far as there is one, cleaves to this hypothesis: for when the fourth commandment was proclaimed from Sinai, and written by the finger of God on one of the stone tables, the reason given for sanctifying the sabbath day is that "in six days the LORD made heaven and earth, the sea, and all that in them is, and rested the seventh day: wherefore the LORD blessed the sabbath day, and hallowed it" [Exod. 20:11]. If the contemplation of the work of creation was the object of setting apart this day, is it not far more reasonable to suppose that it would be observed from the very commencement of the world than that this should commence two thousand years afterwards? The omission of any distinct mention of the sabbath during the period between Adam and Moses, furnishes no argument against the plain interpretation of Genesis 2:2-3; for many other things were omitted in the concise history which we have; and institutions which are regularly observed do not require to be mentioned. Or, if we should suppose that in the wickedness of antediluvian times, this original appointment was neglected, and not revived until Moses, this will account for its omission in the sacred history.

If, then, the sabbath was given to man while in Paradise, it is surely in force ever since; at least, where divine revelation has been enjoyed. It is also a well-ascertained fact that in very ancient times, the seventh day was reckoned sacred among the heathen. The division of the week into seven days among all ancient nations can only be accounted for by supposing an original institution of this kind. That the days of the week were named, among the heathen, from the sun, moon, and planets, does by no means furnish a satisfactory account of the division of time into weeks of seven days. The number of persons who knew anything of the planets was small; and they never could have had influence, from the circumstance that there were seven celestial bodies, to have introduced the division of time into weeks of seven days. The true state of the fact, no doubt, was that this division was received by tradition, as a thing of this kind can be handed down through numerous ages, without the aid of written records. And when the nations turned to idolatry, their principal deities were the sun, moon, and planets; to each of which they assigned a residence, and worshipped them on stated days of the week: in consequence of which, they gave the names of their gods to those days on which they were respectively worshipped.

When the sabbath is first mentioned by Moses, after the exodus, there is no appearance of its being a new institution; but it is referred to as a day accustomed to be observed; or, at least, as one on which it was not lawful to perform the common labors of the week. The mention of it occurs in the account of the descent of the manna. It is said, "On the sixth day, they gathered twice as much bread. And he said unto them, This is that which the Lord hath said, Tomorrow is the rest of the holy sabbath unto the LORD: bake that which ye will bake today, and seethe that ye will seethe; and that which remaineth over lay up for you to be kept until the morning. And they laid it up till the morning, as Moses bade: and it did not stink, neither was there any worm therein. And Moses said, Eat that today; for to-day is a sabbath unto the LORD. So the people rested on the seventh day" [Exodus 16:22, 23-25, 30]. Evidently, this was no part of the ceremonial law, which was not yet given; and no new institution was ever established in this incidental manner. It seems clear that the reference is to a day of rest, of which the people had some knowledge.

The decisive argument for the perpetual obligation of the sabbath is the fourth commandment. The ten commandments, as being of a moral nature, and therefore always binding, were promulgated in a very different manner from the other institutions of Moses. They were first uttered in a voice of thunder, from the midst of the fire on Sinai, and were then inscribed by the finger of God on two tables of hewn stone. Now, it is admitted, that all the other precepts of the Decalogue

are moral; and would it not be an unaccountable thing
that a ceremonial, temporary commandment should be
inserted in the midst of these moral precepts? This is
the law which Christ says he came not to destroy, but
to fulfill. None of these commandments have been
abrogated; and therefore the fourth, as well as the
others, remains in full force. It is remarkable that the
prophets, in denouncing the sins of the people, always
mention the violation of the sabbath in the same
catalogue with the transgression of moral precepts.

It may seem to cursory readers of the New Testament that our Lord abrogated the sabbath, and in His
own conduct disregarded it. But this is far from being
a correct view of the fact. The Pharisees insisted on
such a rigid observation of the day of rest, as to prohibit
works of real necessity and mercy. This superstitious
and overscrupulous opinion, our Savior denounced, and
showed that healing the sick and satisfying the cravings
of hunger were things lawful to be done on the sabbath.
And what renders it certain that this is a correct view
of the matter is that our Lord justifies His conduct by
the practice of the saints in ancient times, when the
sabbath was in full force by the acknowledgment of all,
and by the provisions of the Levitical law itself, which
required the priests to perform double labor on the
sabbath. And He, moreover, showed, that the accusa-
tion against Him, for a violation of the sabbath, was
hypocritical; because, the very persons who made it,
would pull an ox or sheep out of a pit into which it had
fallen, on the sabbath day; and also, because they
thought it no violation of the sacredness of the sabbath,
to lead an ox or ass to watering, though they objected
to the disciples satisfying their hunger on that day.

Our Lord was as much opposed to the perversion of the commandment as to disobedience. He had no respect for the superstitious and unduly rigorous opinions and practices of the self-righteous Pharisees. He taught—and exemplified it in His own conduct—that "the sabbath was made for man, and not man for the sabbath" [Mark 2:27]. One of His expressions has evidently been misunderstood by some interpreters. It is where He says that "the Son of man is Lord also of the sabbath" [Mark 2:28; Luke 6:5]. They have interpreted this to mean that Christ claimed the right to do those things on the sabbath which would be unlawful to others on that day. But this cannot be the meaning; for Christ was made under the law, and had bound Himself to obey it. He came not to destroy the law, but to fulfill it. A breach of the fourth commandment would have been sin in Him, as much as in any other. I take the meaning to be that as He appointed the sabbath, so He best knew how to interpret His own law.

There is a text in Paul's epistle to the Romans which has been supposed to teach that it is a matter of indifference whether we observe the sabbath or not: "One man esteemeth one day above another: another esteemeth every day alike. Let every man be fully persuaded in his own mind" [Rom. 14:5]. But evidently, the question here discussed relates to the ceremonial law. It relates not to the sabbath, which, as we have seen, was no part of the ceremonial law, but belonged to the moral code. The ceremonial law was virtually abrogated by the death of Christ; but all Christians were not yet enlightened to understand their Christian liberty; such indulged in their continued observance of these rites. The apostle is treating here of meats and

drinks and festival days, the binding obligation of
which had ceased.

But in the epistle to the Colossians, Paul says, "Let
no man therefore judge you in meat, or in drink, or in
respect of an holyday, or of the new moon, or of the
sabbath *days*" [Col. 2:16]. Here, again, the ceremonial
law is obviously the subject of discourse. He is speaking
of "meats," "drinks," "new moons," and "sabbath
days." The word *sabbath* relates to the numerous
sabbaths of the ceremonial law, distinct from the
weekly sabbath. Whenever a festival of the law
continued eight days, the first and last were always
kept as sabbaths. Or the reference might be to the
sabbatical year, for the word *days* is not in the original.

But on supposition that the weekly sabbath was
intended, the meaning might be that the Jewish sabbath, namely, the seventh day of the week, was no
longer obligatory on Christians, since they had, by
divine direction, adopted the first day for their day of
sacred rest and of holding public assemblies for the
worship of God. This leads to the inquiry, what evidence do we have that such a change was ever made
by divine authority? The uniform practice of Christians to meet on the first day of the week, from the
very time of Christ's resurrection, is strong evidence
that this change was introduced by Christ and the
apostles. It was suitable that as the worship of God by
His people would have principally respect to the work
of redemption, it should be celebrated on that day on
which it was made manifest that this glorious work
was completed. Accordingly, Christ having risen from
the dead, always met His disciples on this day. And
afterwards, the apostles and the churches were

accustomed to come together on this day, "to break bread" [Acts 20:7], that is, to celebrate the Lord's supper. And when the apostle wrote his first epistle to the Corinthians, it was already established as a custom, not only in the church of Corinth, but in the churches of Macedonia and Galatia, that their contributions for the poor should be collected on this day. From the apostolical practice, we rightly infer the divine authority for this change.

So generally was the first day of the week observed, in commemoration of Christ's resurrection, and for the celebration of religious worship, that in the times of the apostles, it had obtained the significant denomination of the *Lord's day*. That this appellation really was applied to the first day of the week by the apostle John in the Apocalypse is evident, because it can, with no appearance of reason, be applied to any other day; and also, because this became a common appellation of that day among Christians in all subsequent ages to this time, as appears by the testimony of Justin Martyr and others.

It may still seem strange to some that, if the fourth commandment was of perpetual obligation, it should never have been expressly inculcated in the New Testament, nor the violation of this precept be placed in the many catalogues of immoralities found in the writings of the apostles.

To remove this difficulty, it may be observed that without a divine revelation, the heathen could not know what portion of time, or what particular day should be observed. They were bound to appropriate a due proportion of time to the worship of God, but what that proportion should be, reason could not determine. It can scarcely be considered, therefore, that they sinned in not observing the sabbath. Though this is, by the prophets, always charged on the Jews as a great sin, yet they do not denounce the Gentiles on account of their neglect of the sabbath. Yet such strangers as lived in Judea were bound to regard this day.

Again, at the time of our Savior's advent, the external violation of the sabbath was not common among the Jews; but, on the contrary, their principal teachers —the Scribes and Pharisees—had inculcated a degree of rigor in keeping the sabbath that was contrary to its design, which superstition our Lord condemned, and showed both by His discourses and His actions, that the sabbath was made for man, and not man for the sabbath.

In regard to converts to Christianity from among the heathen, they would be so desirous to hear the Word, and attend on the ordinances which were administered on this day, that they stood in no need of admonition on this subject. When any, however, began to grow cold, and to decline in their religious zeal, as was the case with many of the Hebrews, to whom Paul wrote, they also began to neglect the public assemblies, which were held on this day, and were admonished, by the apostle, in the following words: "Not forsaking the assembling of yourselves together, as the manner of some is" [Heb. 10:25].

Unless we had a particular day set apart by divine authority for the worship of God, this important duty could never be performed in an edifying manner; public worship would, for the most part, fall into disuse. And if a certain day should be agreed upon by the church, or by the civil government, it would lack that authority and sanctity which are necessary to its general observance. As it is, we find how difficult it is to get men to cease from their earthly cares and pursuits on this day, although it has been demonstrated that they are rather losers than gainers, even in a worldly point of view, by the breach of this holy commandment. It was, therefore, wisely placed among the most binding precepts of the moral law.

It is unnecessary to dilate on the manifold blessings which the institution of the sabbath confers on man. This has been done, of late, in the clearest manner, by a reference to facts, derived in part from the experience of worldly men.

This chapter shall, therefore, be concluded with a few directions for the observance of the Lord's day.

1. Let the whole day be consecrated to the service of God, especially in acts of worship, public and private. This weekly recess from worldly cares and avocations, affords a precious opportunity for the study of God's Word, and for the examination of our own hearts. Rise early, and let your first thoughts and aspirations be directed to heaven. Meditate much and profoundly on divine things, and endeavor to acquire a degree of spirituality on this day which will abide with you through the whole week.

2. Consider the Lord's day an honor and delight. Let your heart be elevated in holy joy, and your lips be employed in the high praises of God. This day more resembles heaven than any other portion of our time, and we should endeavor to imitate the worship of heaven, according to that petition of the Lord's prayer—"Thy will be done on earth as it is in heaven" [Matt. 6:10]. Never permit the idea to enter your mind that the sabbath is a burden. It is a sad case when professing

Christians are weary of this sacred rest, and say, like some of old, "When will the new moon be gone, that we may sell corn? and the sabbath, that we may set forth wheat?" [Amos 8:5]. As you improve this day, so probably you will prosper all the week.

3. Avoid undue rigor, and Pharisaic scrupulosity, for nothing renders the Lord's day more odious. Still keep in view the great end of its institution; and remember that the sabbath was instituted for the benefit of man, and not to be a galling yoke. The cessation from worldly business and labor is not for its own sake, as if there was anything morally good in inaction, but we are called off from secular pursuits on this day, that we may have a portion of our time to devote uninterruptedly to the worship of God. Let everything then be so arranged in your household beforehand, that there may be no interruption to religious duties, and to attendance on the means of grace. There was undoubtedly a rigor in the law of the sabbath, as given to the Jews, which did not exist before; and which does not apply to Christians. They were forbidden to kindle a fire, or to go out of their place on the sabbath; and for gathering a few sticks, a presumptuous transgressor was stoned to death. These regulations are not now in force.

As divine knowledge is the richest acquisition within our reach, and as this knowledge is to be found in the Word of God, let us value this day as affording all persons an opportunity of hearing and reading the Word. As the fourth commandment requires the heads of families to cause the sabbath to be observed by all under their control, or within their gates, it is very important that domestic and culinary arrangements should be so ordered that servants and domestics should not be deprived of the opportunity of attending on the Word and worship of God which this day affords, by being employed in preparing superfluous feasts, as is often the case. The sabbath is more valuable to the poor and unlearned than to others, because it is almost the only leisure which they have, and because means of public instruction are on that day afforded them by the preaching of the gospel. If we possess any measure of the true spirit of devotion, this sacred day will be most welcome to our hearts; and we will rejoice when they say, "Let us go into the house of the LORD" [Ps. 122:1]. To such a soul, the opportunity of enjoying spiritual communion with God will be valued above all price, and be esteemed as the richest privilege which creatures can enjoy upon earth.

4. While you conscientiously follow your own sense of duty in the observance of the rest of the sabbath, be not ready to censure all who may differ from you in regard to minute particulars, which are not prescribed or commanded in the Word of God. The Jews accused our Lord as a sabbath-breaker on many occasions, and would have put Him to death for a supposed violation of this law, had He not escaped out of their hands. Beware of indulging yourself in any practice which may have the effect of leading others to disregard the rest and sanctity of the sabbath. Let not your liberty in regard to what you think may be done, be a stumbling-block to cause weaker brethren to offend, or unnecessarily to give them pain, or to lead them to entertain an unfavorable opinion of your piety.

5. As, undoubtedly, the celebration of public worship and gaining divine instruction from the divine oracles, is the main object of the institution of the Christian

sabbath, let all be careful to attend on the services of the sanctuary on this day. And let the heart be prepared by previous prayer and meditation for a participation in public worship, and while in the more immediate presence of the Divine Majesty, let all the people fear before Him, and with reverence adore and praise His holy name. Let all vanity, curious gazing, and slothfulness, be banished from the house of God. Let every heart be lifted up on entering the sanctuary, and let the thoughts be carefully restrained from wandering on foolish or worldly objects, and resolutely recalled when they have begun to go astray. Let brotherly love be cherished, when joining with others in the worship of God. The hearts of all the church should be united in worship, as the heart of one man. Thus will the worship of the sanctuary below be a preparation for the purer, sublimer worship in the temple above.

CHAPTER 34

Death

All the doctrines and duties of religion have relation to a future state. All religion is founded on the supposition that man will live after the death of the body. The importance of any doctrine or religious institution, depends very much on its bearing on the future destinies of men. Religion, therefore, teaches its votaries to be much occupied with the contemplation of the unseen world. It is especially the province of faith to fix the attention of the mind on these awful but invisible realities, and by this means to draw off the too eager affections from the objects of the present world. Of whatever else men may doubt, they cannot be skeptical in regard to death. The evidences of the certainty of this event to all are so multiplied and so frequently obtruded on our attention, that all know that it is appointed for them once to die; and yet, notwithstanding this certainty and the frequent mementos which we have, most men are but slightly impressed with their mortality until death actually comes near, and eternity, with its awful realities, begins to open before them.

Death is, according to Scripture, "the wages of sin" [Rom. 6:23]. By sin death entered into the world. The death of the body is a part of the punishment of sin; except in the case of the believer, who is freed from the condemnation of the law, and to whom death, though frightful and painful, is no curse, but rather a blessing. For by the death of Christ as his Surety, the penalty of the law has been exhausted. "There is therefore now no condemnation to them which are in Christ Jesus" [Rom. 8:1]. To them "to die is gain" [Phil. 1:21]. To them, the monster has no sting. To them, death is a deliverance from sin and suffering, and an entrance into perfect holiness and happiness. As soon as the true Christian departs, he is with Christ, and is like Him, and beholds His glory. Therefore, Paul in his inventory of the rich possessions of the saints, reckons death as one: "For all things are yours; whether Paul, or Apollos, or Cephas, or the world, or life, or death, or things present, or things to come; all are yours; and ye are Christ's; and Christ is God's" [1 Cor. 3:21-23].

All we know of death is that it is a separation of the soul from the body; the consequence of which to the latter is an immediate disorganization and corruption. As it was taken from the dust, so it returns to dust again. But as to the soul, being essentially living and active, it continues its conscious exercises, but in what way, when deprived of its usual organs, we cannot tell. As all our experience has been in connection with bodily organs, we of course can know nothing of the exercises of mind in a state where no such organs are possessed. All attempts, therefore, to imagine what the condition of the soul in a separate state is, must be vain.

But we need not be perplexed or troubled on account of our ignorance of the future state. We may well trust, in this case, as in others, our divine Redeemer and faithful Friend to arrange all matters for His own glory and for our benefit. The gracious declaration that "all things work together for good to them that love

God, who are the called according to his purpose"
[Rom. 8:28], is not only true in relation to their pilgrimage on earth, but also in regard to their passage
through the valley of the shadow of death. Thus, they
need fear no evil, for the great Shepherd has promised
to be with them and to comfort them, with His rod and
His staff. "My flesh and my heart faileth: but God is
the strength of my heart, and my portion for ever" [Ps.
73:26]. "Precious in the sight of the Lord is the death
of his saints" [Ps. 116:15].

Although little is revealed respecting the mode of existence and enjoyment in a separate state, for the plain
reason that no description could be understood by us,
yet we may confidently trust our blessed Redeemer to
provide for the guidance and comfort of the soul, when
it enters an unknown world. When Lazarus died, angels
stood ready to receive and convoy his departing spirit;
and we have no reason to think that this favor was
peculiar to this saint; but rather that it was recorded in
this instance to teach us that the same might be
expected in every case of the death of a true believer.

CHAPTER 35

The Resurrection

Leaving, therefore, the intermediate state between death and judgment, in that obscurity in which revelation has left it, let us proceed, briefly to contemplate those important events connected with our future existence, concerning which the Scriptures speak plainly—I mean the resurrection and judgment. The redemption purchased by the merit and death of Christ respects the body as well as the soul. The redemption of the body is one of those things for which believers wait in hope. Although the threatening that unto dust it shall return will be verified, yet the body itself shall rise again. Christ is "the resurrection and the life" [John 11:25]. "For," said Christ to the Jews, "the hour is coming, in the which all that are in the graves shall hear his voice, and shall come forth; they that have done good, unto the resurrection of life; and they that have done evil, unto the resurrection of damnation" [John 5:28-29]. "Since by man came death, by man came also the resurrection of the dead. For as in Adam all die, even so in Christ shall all be made alive" [1 Cor. 15:21-22]. "Knowing that he which raised up the Lord Jesus shall raise up us also by Jesus" [2 Cor. 4:14].

When it is asserted that all must die and be raised again, those must be excepted who shall be alive upon the earth when Christ shall come; for, "behold," says

Paul, "I show you a mystery; we shall not all sleep, but we shall all be changed, in a moment, in the twinkling of an eye, at the last trump" [1 Cor. 15:51-52]. "For the Lord himself shall descend from heaven with a shout, with the voice of the archangel, and with the trump of God: and the dead in Christ shall rise first: then we which are alive and remain shall be caught up together with them in the clouds, to meet the Lord in the air: and so shall we ever be with the Lord" [1 Thess. 4:16-17].

As to the difficulties which reason may suggest in regard to the resurrection of the same body, we need give ourselves no trouble. Let us believe that with God all things are possible, and "that, what he had promised, he was able also to perform" [Rom. 4:21]. "Why," says Paul, in his speech before Agrippa, "why should it be thought a thing incredible with you, that God should raise the dead?" [Acts 26:8].

CHAPTER 36

The Judgment

Immediately after the resurrection comes the judgment of men and devils. The time of this event is called the *last day*, and the *day of judgment* (2 Pet. 3:7). "Because he hath appointed a day, in the which he will judge the world in righteousness by that man whom he hath ordained" (Acts 17:31). "It is appointed unto men once to die, but after this the judgment" (Heb. 9:27). "For we must all appear before the judgment seat of Christ; that every one may receive the things done in his body, according to that he hath done, whether it be good or bad" (2 Cor. 5:10). "I charge thee therefore before God, and the Lord Jesus Christ, who shall judge the quick and the dead at his appearing and his kingdom" (2 Tim. 4:1). "And the angels which kept not their first estate, but left their own habitation, he hath reserved in everlasting chains under darkness unto the judgment of the great day" (Jude 6). "For God shall bring every work into judgment, with every secret thing, whether it be good, or whether it be evil" (Eccles. 12:14).

The end of appointing a day of judgment is, that the justice of God may be manifested in His treatment of His creatures, and that the righteous may be vindicated from all those calumnies which were heaped upon them in this world. When the conduct of the wicked shall be disclosed and all their secret motives and purposes brought to light, it will be manifest to the whole universe that their condemnation is just, and especially, when it is seen that punishment is exactly proportioned to the guilt of the offender. But the degree of guilt will not be measured by the enormity of the outward act alone; the light and privileges enjoyed by some will give such crimson color to their crimes that their punishment will be greater than that of much more atrocious sinners, who lived in ignorance of the truths of God. This accords with the woe pronounced by our Savior against Chorazin, Bethsaida, and Capernaum, when He said that it will be more tolerable for Tyre and Sidon in the day of judgment than for the first two cities, and more tolerable for Sodom than for the last.

Everyone must perceive the fitness of appointing Christ to be the Judge, since all power in heaven and earth is committed unto Him, and He is made head over all things to His church. As He was arraigned at a human tribunal and unjustly condemned, it is suitable that His enemies should behold Him on the throne of His glory. It is on many accounts suitable that they who pierced Him should see Him coming in the clouds of heaven; and that all those who conspired His death, and who with wicked hands crucified the Prince of life, should be brought to answer for their atrocious crimes at the tribunal of Him whom they maliciously accused, unjustly condemned, and cruelly put to death.

Another reason why God manifest in the flesh should be constituted Judge of quick and dead is that He can appear visibly in His proper person, which the Father cannot. As His disciples can only be pronounced acquitted on account of His perfect righteousness, it is altogether suitable that He should be on the judgment seat to acknowledge them. Their conduct will also be exhibited, not as answering the demands of the law, but as evidence of their sincere faith in His name, and because the reward bestowed on them will be measured by their good works. Whether their secret sins will on that day be brought to light has been disputed; but since the glory of the Redeemer will be enhanced in proportion to the guilt and misery of the redeemed, there is no solid reason why the sins of believers should be kept secret, especially as many of their sins must be known even to the wicked. Those texts which speak of the sins of God's people as blotted out, as buried in the sea, as covered, etc., do all relate to the pardon of sin, not to their being concealed on the day of judgment.

CHAPTER 37

Heaven, or the State of Glorification

Some things are hard to be believed because they are so good and glorious. That such poor, ignorant, imperfect, and unworthy creatures, should ever arrive at a state, in which they shall know as they are known [1 Cor. 13:12], and shall be free from all imperfection in their moral exercises and be continually as happy as they are capable of being, is hard for us in our present state distinctly to conceive of. Therefore the glorious realities of another world make, commonly, but a feeble impression on the minds of Christians. Perhaps a more deep and vivid impression of the nearness and glory of the heavenly state would so absorb their minds as to render them unfit to perform the common business of this life. It is, however, exceedingly desirable that the children of God should think more of the heavenly state, and have a more habitual impression of the felicity and purity of the celestial world than they commonly possess. In this brief summary, our object shall be, in the simplest manner, to exhibit, without exaggeration or amplification, what is revealed in the sacred Scriptures respecting the condition of the righteous after the judgment is brought to a close. May the Spirit of God enlighten our blind minds to perceive the reality, felicity, and glory of the heavenly state.

The righteous, at the day of judgment, will be openly acknowledged and acquitted; and shall receive from the Judge a gracious welcome into His kingdom and glory; for "then shall the King say unto them on his right hand, Come, ye blessed of my Father, inherit the kingdom prepared for you from the foundation of the world" [Matt. 25:34]. Their minds will, no doubt, be wonderfully enlarged; and it is no extravagant idea, and is altogether consistent with analogy, to suppose that we have now in our mental constitution the germ of faculties which have never been developed in this world, because here their exercise was not needed; but which, upon our transition into the celestial world, will be brought into full activity, and will qualify us to participate in the social intercourse and employments of the heavenly state. There, the glorious attributes of God will be clearly exhibited to the understanding. There, the whole current of the affections will be concentrated on Christ, through whom the Father manifests Himself. There, every desire, every volition, every thought, will be in conformity with the divine will. Nothing will be lacking to that perfection of sublime and pure enjoyment, of which each individual is capable; for although the happiness of everyone will be complete, yet there will be many degrees, as some will have larger capacities than others; as many vessels of different dimensions cast into the sea will all be full, yet their contents may be vastly different.

As all rational happiness is founded in knowledge of objects suited to satisfy and fill the rational mind, it is reasonable to think that in heaven there will be a gradual progress in knowledge; and as the object, even the divine attributes, is infinite, this progress may, indeed must, go on progressively through eternity. Hence we can understand why it is that the joys of heaven admit of no alloy from their long continuance, or constant repetition. New and interesting discoveries of celestial objects will furnish continual novelty and variety to entertain the spiritual taste of the rational mind.

The exercise of the social affections will be a source of pure and unspeakable felicity. There, no envious, narrow, or selfish feelings will exist to interrupt the sweet communion of kindred spirits. The unity and harmony of spirit in the continual praise of God will be a source of the most pure and elevated enjoyment, far above what tongue can express or heart conceive. There, indeed, all believers will be melted down, as it were, into one and will constitute one glorious body, Christ being the Head.

The bodies of the saints will be exactly suited to the celestial world, and its delights and employments. These bodies of flesh and blood, created from the dust, will be so changed at the resurrection that they will be fashioned like unto Christ's body, which undoubtedly is the most glorious visible object in the universe. It would be vain and presumptuous for us to imagine what will be the structure, the organs, and the habiliments of the glorified bodies of the saints. The nearest approximation that we can make to a conception of this matter, will consist merely in removing from our minds all those weaknesses and imperfections which cleave to these earthly bodies. Paul has, with the pen of inspiration, written nothing more sublime than in his discourse respecting the resurrection of the bodies

216 A Brief Compendium of Bible Truth

of the saints: "It is sown in corruption; it is raised in incorruption: it is sown in dishonour; it is raised in glory: it is sown in weakness; it is raised in power: it is sown a natural body; it is raised a spiritual body" (1 Cor. 15:42-44). Further on, the apostle adds, "So when this corruptible shall have put on incorruption, and this mortal shall have put on immortality, then shall be brought to pass the saying that is written, Death is swallowed up in victory" [1 Cor. 15:54]. In heaven there is no sickness, no tears, no death, no sin, no weariness, no alloy, no sleep, no fear; but everlasting joy and glory shall crown the heads of the redeemed. This felicity will not only be uninterrupted, but eternal in its duration; for while the wicked shall go away into everlasting punishment the righteous shall go into life eternal.

CHAPTER 38

Hell, or the State of Future Misery

The most incomprehensible of all mysteries is that moral evil should have a place in the universe of an infinitely wise, holy, and powerful God. We could construct a very plausible argument, *a priori*, to prove from the above premises, that moral evil never could be permitted to exist in the world. But how futile are all reasonings against facts experienced every moment and by every man. The philosopher who undertook to demonstrate that there could be no such thing as motion, received the right answer when the person addressed uttered not a word, but rose up and walked. So we may answer all arguments against the possibility of the existence of evil by pointing to the prison, the hospital, and the grave. We need not go so far; we need only refer the sophist to his own experience. Now, if moral evil has an existence, it is evident that pain or natural evil must follow. No conviction of the human mind is clearer or stronger than that crime should be visited by punishment. Every judgment of the moral faculty, every feeling of disapprobation at unprovoked injury, every twinge of remorse, furnishes indubitable proof that moral evil should be visited with punishment. From this law, written on the heart, no man can escape. "The wages of sin is death" [Rom. 6:23] and the very practice of moral evil involves misery in the very exercise.

Some who cannot but admit that moral evil exists, and that as long as it does exist, there must be misery, yet cannot be reconciled to the doctrine of eternal misery, which seems to be clearly taught in the Word of God. That any of God's rational creatures should be doomed to a state of everlasting sin and misery is indeed an appalling idea, from which the benevolent sympathetic mind would gladly shrink; but as far as reason is concerned, the chief difficulty is admitted when it is conceded that sin and misery have an actual existence in the world, and have had from a period near its commencement. For if evil may exist, as it has done, consistent with the divine attributes, it may exist hereafter—it may exist forever. When it is argued that sin cannot deserve such a punishment, something is assumed which cannot be known to be true. If sin may exist and be punished for ages, no man can prove that it may not exist forever, and forever be the cause of misery. The idea is indeed so painful to our feelings that unless the will of God had been revealed too clearly to be mistaken, the doctrine of eternal misery would never have been received by any considerable number of persons; but revolting as it is to our sensibilities, it has been from the beginning the belief of the whole Christian church with a very few exceptions. We believe this doctrine, simply because we find it plainly written in innumerable passages of Scripture. If there is any art by which this array of testimony can be set aside, then it will be a legitimate inference that no doctrine is or can be proved from the sacred Word.

It is not intended to adduce all the Scripture proofs of this awful doctrine. They may be met with on almost every page of the New Testament. It may not be amiss, however, to cite a few passages, that the reader may have a specimen of the proof texts which may be adduced. There is a sin for which there is no forgiveness, neither in this world nor in the world to come. There was a person, concerning whom our Savior said, it had been good for him if he had never been born; which can only be true on the supposition that punishment will be eternal. There were some of whom Christ said, "Ye shall die in your sins [John 8:24], and where I am thither ye cannot come" [John 7:34]. It is said, that many "will seek to enter in, and shall not be able" [Luke 13:24].

Besides, we have not the least intimation that the lost can ever be rendered meet for the heavenly state. Certainly, the society and blasphemy of devils have no tendency to fit the souls of the damned for the pure joys of the celestial world. And, in confirmation of the common doctrine, we have in Scripture every form of expression which could express eternity of misery. The same terms which are employed to teach the eternal existence of God and the perpetuity of the happiness of the righteous, are also used to teach the endless sufferings of the finally impenitent. And, for aught we know, eternity is an immutable state of existence; he who is doomed to punishment in another world must suffer eternally, because the successions of time have no existence there.

We are not more certainly assured of the perpetuity of future misery than of the intensity of the torments which must be endured by the wretched creatures who shall be doomed to everlasting banishment from the comfortable presence of God. Whether the fire of hell is a material fire, is an inquiry of no importance. It matters not whether excruciating pain proceeds from a material or immaterial cause. The misery of lost sinners must be inconceivably dreadful, if they should be abandoned to their own feelings of remorse, despair, and the raging of malignant passions, then free from all restraint. This state of misery is spoken of as a place of outer darkness; a lake of fire and brimstone. It is a place where the worm dieth not, and where the fire is not quenched. Let every one who is within the reach of mercy flee from the coming wrath, and take refuge under the outstretched wings of *divine mercy*.